Are You Drifting?

TIM RODE

BALBOA.
PRESS

A DIVISION OF HAY HOUSE

Balboa Press books may be ordered through booksellers or by contacting:

Balboa Press
A Division of Hay House
1663 Liberty Drive
Bloomington, IN 47403
www.balboapress.com
1 (877) 407-4847

Because of the dynamic nature of the Internet, any web addresses or
links contained in this book may have changed since publication and
may no longer be valid. The views expressed in this work are solely those
of the author and do not necessarily reflect the views of the publisher,
and the publisher hereby disclaims any responsibility for them.

The author of this book does not dispense medical advice or prescribe the use
of any technique as a form of treatment for physical, emotional, or medical
problems without the advice of a physician, either directly or indirectly. The
intent of the author is only to offer information of a general nature to help
you in your quest for emotional and spiritual well-being. In the event you use
any of the information in this book for yourself, which is your constitutional
right, the author and the publisher assume no responsibility for your actions.

Any people depicted in stock imagery provided by Thinkstock are
models, and such images are being used for illustrative purposes only.
Certain stock imagery © Thinkstock.

Printed in the United States of America.

ISBN: 978-1-4525-8806-3 (sc)
ISBN: 978-1-4525-8808-7 (hc)
ISBN: 978-1-4525-8807-0 (e)

Library of Congress Control Number: 2013922377

Balboa Press rev. date: 12/30/2013

Contents

Introduction

It is not the author who creates the book, but the book that creates
the author, just as we all are creations of the mental images and
ideas and thoughts that have found a home in our minds.[1]
—U. S. Andersen

To drift or not to drift? That is the question you will need to ask
yourself. Are you drifting in your life? Are you just going through
the motions, doing the same things day in and day out? The same
routine that you have followed for years? If so, maybe it's time for
a wake-up call. Maybe you need to take the advice of the Greek
philosopher Heraclitus: "Every walking animal is driven to its
purpose with a whack."[2] Maybe it's time for a good whack. Deep
down, you know that you have a much greater purpose, much
loftier goals and aspirations, but yet you continue to drift.

Or are you the type of person who has to be constantly on
the go? Do you plan every minute of your day from the time you
wake up until your head hits the pillow at night? You have no time
for yourself, as you are constantly *doing* all day long. If you are
this type of person, you may *need* to drift. As you will see in the
pages that follow, drifting can be not only a time to recuperate and
revitalize, but also a time when your mind is still and more likely
to be creative and original, a time to let your true genius surface.

This book is about incorporating both *drifting* and *not drifting* into your life. It's about bringing awareness to your life now and perhaps motivating yourself to do something different.

I have read hundreds of business, inspirational, metaphysical, and philosophical books, and this book contains some of the best excerpts, passages, and quotes from my favorite books and authors on a wide variety of topics that are of interest to me and hopefully to you as well. My intention is to make you aware that there is another way of looking at life and the things you believe in. Look at your life now and determine if you are just going through the motions with no purpose or maybe need to slow down and stop the constant *doing*. Perhaps you are satisfied with your life and feel you don't need to change anything. Whatever your life situation, this book is ultimately about your personal freedom.

The ideas and concepts in this book may expose you to freedoms you never knew existed. Although most of us think we want happiness in life—and there are countless books on the shelves promising to tell us how to get it—I believe that what we are really longing for is freedom. If you make freedom your ultimate purpose in life, you won't have to worry about chasing the elusive happiness that is here one minute and gone the next.

If I had to sum up what my life mission has been, it wouldn't be school, grades, college, athletics, career… no, it would be my lifelong quest for freedom. It's my passion. The pursuit of freedom is the reason for everything in my life. But the question has always been, "Free from what?" By the end of this book, I hope you will know, and I hope that you too can find freedom in your life. You will see how this pursuit of freedom has influenced almost every aspect of my life—and almost always for the better.

As I mentioned, there are a wide variety of topics and ideas in this book, and if you find one that doesn't resonate with you, move on to the next. I chose to use and share some of the best teachings that I have read on topics that I feel passionate about and that I believe will benefit you as well. This book contains what I consider the "best of the best," with excerpts and writings from a wide variety of authors, sages, and inspirational teachers. The book also contains many quotes. I love quotes, not only for their timeless message but also for their simplicity.

Finally, you may be wondering, what qualifies me to write a book? A better question might be, *why* would I want to write a book? I have a successful business, so it's not for the money. It's not for the travel, as the only traveling I like to do now is to my favorite vacation destinations.

So what qualifies me to write this book? The best answer I can come up with is a burning desire deep within to put on paper that which has been in my head for the past ten years. Each day that goes by in which I have done little or no writing, I have the same feeling I used to get in school when I knew I had homework or a test to study for but put it off. I feel the same way about this book that I did over twenty years ago when I started the company, TR Toppers, that I currently own with my two brothers.

A business I started with a simple idea, a knife, a bucket, and some Reese's Peanut Butter Cups is now a successful company, distributing chopped candy toppings throughout the country with sales over 100 million dollars. Many people have good ideas, but the key here is that I took action. I had drifted long enough. I mention the sales not to boast but to show the magnitude of the business that I started at a time in my life when I had virtually no money. My first child was on the way, I owned frozen-yogurt shops with rapidly declining sales, and I was closing in on my personal rock bottom. You can read more about that in chapter 9, "The Beauty of Rock Bottom."

So back to the question: what qualifies me to write a book?

> If man carries within him any portion of that which is
> infinite and eternal, then it becomes his obligation to
> express it. If he does not, he loses his soul. That which
> is unexpressed, in the end becomes non-existent.[3]
> —U. S. Andersen

I have been carrying this book around in my mind and my soul for many years, and I now feel it is my obligation to express it, otherwise I *would* lose a part of my soul, and in the end it would be nonexistent. So am I qualified to write a book? Lord Byron wrote, "One hates an author that's all author."[4] That offers hope! I feel the words of Robert Lowell can answer if I am qualified much more eloquently than I possibly could:

> I'm sure that writing isn't a craft, that is, something
> for which you learn the skills and go on turning out. It
> must come from some deep impulse, deep inspiration.
> That can't be taught, it can't be what you use in teaching.[5]

This book is my deep impulse, my deep inspiration.

1

To Drift?

We are never without a pilot. When we know not how to steer,
and dare not hoist a sail, we can drift… The ship of heaven
guides itself, and will not accept a wooden rudder.[6]
—Ralph Waldo Emerson

U. S. Andersen writes in his book *The Magic in Your Mind*,
"Shakespeare's Hamlet in his famed soliloquy pondered, 'To
be or not to be,' and thus faced squarely the primary challenge
of life. Most people only exist, never truly *are* at all. They exist
as predictable equations, reacting rather than acting, walking
compendiums of aphorisms and taboos, reflexes and syndromes.
Surely the gods must chuckle at the ironic spectacle of robots
fancying themselves free, but still, when finally the embodied
consciousness rises above the pain-pleasure principle of nature,
the true meaning of freedom is made apparent at last."[7]

We all exist to some extent in the manner that Andersen
describes, as mechanical robots reacting to everything life throws
our way—reacting, overreacting, consumed by all the external
happenings in our life, living life entirely by our five senses. The
question we have to ask ourselves is, how long are we going to live

like this? How long are we going to be mechanical robots? How long are we going to drift through life? Without question, I have had far more times of drifting in my life than times of action. I think this holds true for most of us. Many of you may be offended by this statement and feel that you have no time to drift, that you work hard, that you are always busy, and that drifting is the last thing you'd have time for.

But even though much of your "busyness" may be necessary, it could also be considered a form of drifting. The reason I say this is because in most cases, very little creativity comes forth when you are constantly *doing*. Your mind is preoccupied with all the things you have to do. The never-ending to-do list in your mind is always unfurling.

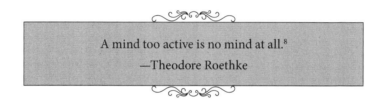

A mind too active is no mind at all.[8]
—Theodore Roethke

In Christian McEwen's book *World Enough and Time*, writing about the artist Paulus Berensohn, the artist is quoted as saying, "'Creativity can be very fast and very spontaneous.' But first there had to be time to dream and drift, to listen and attend. 'Imagination comes into us before it comes out of us. It is a receptive, a feminine process… imagination for me requires slowness; *slow and savor.*'"[9]

It's easy to fall into this trap of *doing*. It makes you feel productive accomplishing daily tasks, checking items off your to-do list, running from here to there at a frantic pace, always racing the clock to get things done. We all do this, and it is a necessary part of life.

There is also a feeling of importance that comes along with being busy. *I must be an important person, because I am so busy.* You hear it all the time: "I'm too busy now." "I don't have time to do that." "I'm crazy busy." You receive Christmas letters from people who talk about how busy they have been the past year and how quickly the year went by. The primary message for the entire year is how busy they were.

Obviously, it would be a pretty boring Christmas message if they wrote about how they drifted all year and did absolutely nothing! But drifting and slowing down are also a necessary part of life, and we all need that. It is during this drifting or slowing-down time that creativity and genius will surface. It's a time to let your mind be still and open to universal intelligence.

We all have things we have to do, and as you will read in the next chapter, busyness and taking action are necessary if you ever want to fulfill your dreams and desires. But slowing down, taking time for yourself, being alone, drifting, will give you access to your greatest powers, ideas, revelations, and creativity.

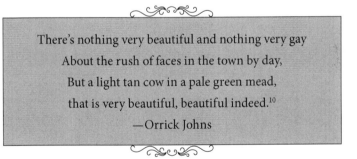

There's nothing very beautiful and nothing very gay
About the rush of faces in the town by day,
But a light tan cow in a pale green mead,
that is very beautiful, beautiful indeed.[10]
—Orrick Johns

How often have you heard someone say, "I know you're busy, but… can I take a few minutes of your time?" That one really makes you feel important. *I am so busy that I can't give someone else any of my time!* How special does that make you feel? *I can't give another person any of my time because it is far too valuable, and I am too important!*

I have employees come into my office all the time who say this very thing: "I know you're very busy, but…" and I always tell them, "No, I am not busy." As a matter of fact, I am probably the least busy person in the company. But I don't tell them *that*!

It is rare now to find anyone in an airport who isn't talking on a cell phone, texting, checking e-mails—all way too busy to have any idle time, any time to pause and reflect. To observe. To take in the sights, the sounds, the beauty. Today's technology has given us a way to escape the present moment. It's like an addiction, and if you took away the toys, what would the addict do? Alone with yourself and your thoughts! Could there be any worse punishment? And yet, as will be shown, this is the place you need to go. It's where all your creativity arises, where the greatest ideas and thoughts come from.

Dr. Joseph Murphy, in his book *The Miracles of Your Mind*, writes that author "Elbert Hubbard declared that his most important ideas came while he was relaxed, or working in the garden, or going for a walk; the reason being when the conscious mind is relaxed, the subjective wisdom comes to the fore. There are oftentimes inspirational uprushes when the conscious mind is completely relaxed."[11]

Today's technology is a wonderful tool and has given us access and the ability to work from an airport or almost anywhere in the world. When I am in the airport, I do the same thing. I use my cell phone, check e-mails—it's a great place to get caught up on your work. But I also spend time doing nothing. Don't be afraid to sit quietly and observe. Walk the terminal with no agenda. The answers you were looking for on a particular business problem or personal issue may come to you as you stroll through the airport with nothing on your mind. You may come up with the perfect response for an e-mail that's been troubling you. And even though you may feel that you are not being productive because you aren't checking e-mails, texting, or talking on your cell phone, you might be pleasantly surprised at the revelations that come to you.

Take time to be bored. One time I heard a coworker say, "When I get busy, I get stupid." Ain't that the truth. Creative people need time to just sit around and do nothing. I get some of my best ideas when I'm bored, which is why I never take my shirts to the cleaners. I love ironing my shirts—it's so boring, I almost always get good ideas. If you're out of ideas, wash the dishes. Take a really long walk. Stare at a spot on the wall for as long as you can. As the artist Maira Kalman says, "Avoiding work is the way to focus my mind."

Take time to mess around. Get lost. Wander. You never know where it's going to lead you."[12]

—Austin Kleon, *Steal Like An Artist*

I am not telling you this so that you will drop everything and start drifting through life. There is nothing wrong with being on the go, talking on your cell phone, running errands, taking care of life. We all have things we have to do, and despite how boring or mundane they may seem, they still need to get done. I do the same thing every day. But rarely does anything great ever come to us when we are constantly *doing*.

> All search for power is done with the ego,
> with the thought, "I am doing."[13]
> —Papaji

Now, if you are working on a project, business idea, work-related project, book, painting, athletic endeavor, pursuit of a dream, and you are *busy* and *doing* for the sake of trying to make your dream a reality, that is not drifting. From my perspective, there are three types of drifting. Two you might want to avoid, but the third may work to your advantage.

The first type of drifting is being an actual *drifter*. In this country, such individuals may also go by the name of vagabond, bum, or homeless. Many of these drifters are forced into a life of drifting because of life circumstances. There are obviously many reasons why people find themselves in this position (joblessness, no family, health issues, mental illness). And there also may be a few who have chosen this lifestyle—a lifestyle in which they report to no one and have no boss. To them, it may be their freedom.

Eastern cultures have monks, sages, yogis, and gurus. These people could also be viewed as drifters, especially from the viewpoint of Western culture. Most Eastern drifters have chosen their lifestyle, many on a quest to seek enlightenment. They understand there is a need for stillness, to be alone, to meditate. It is their lifelong quest. And maybe some of the drifters in this country are also on a personal journey of enlightenment, despite not being in a cave or sitting in the lotus position. Eckhart Tolle, author of *The Power of Now* and other great works, spent two years sitting on a park bench before he was "enlightened." He gave up what seemed to be a fruitful career in academia to sit on a park bench. For two years! That is one serious meditation session. He may have been one of the lucky ones in that it only took two years, whereas for many drifters, it takes a lifetime. Or maybe they are the lucky ones?

True intelligence operates silently—
stillness is where creativity and solutions to problems are.[14]
—Eckhart Tolle

This book is not about critiquing lifestyles. We are all free (if we know it) to choose whatever we want to do with our lives. It's one of the greatest freedoms we have. I will say that there is an element of freedom that drifters have in their lives that has always been intriguing and fascinating to me. I think it would make an interesting book to go to different cities throughout the country and interview some of these drifters to find out if they were forced into a life of drifting or chose it themselves. As an entrepreneur and a risk-taker, I have always felt there is a fine line between being successful and being on the streets with my fellow drifters.

The second type of drifting is being constantly on the go, doing the same habitual things that you do every day—never taking time for yourself, an endless *doing* all day long. Even though you may feel that you are successful, have provided for your family, have a nice home, new cars, and a decent job, deep down there is something in you that wants something different, something greater. But you have fallen into the belief that this is your lot in life, your destiny, the way it's meant to be, and that you are unable to control your fate. You are drifting through life. By all outward appearances, you seem to be successful, but on the inside there is a burning desire for something different. You want something different and better, but you just keep drifting.

The third type of drifting—and the drifting that I feel is not only necessary but the most important form of drifting—is the time we take for ourselves because we know there is more to life than what we have experienced so far, that we want something far greater. We know we have this greatness in us but are not sure how to bring it out. This type of drifting is why we take sabbaticals from work, retreats, leaves of absence, time away. It's a time to reflect and contemplate life, to meditate. It's a time to discover your true dreams and desires instead of those imposed on you. To experience solitude. To be quiet. To "be still, and know that I am God." (Psalm 46:10). It's a time for your greatest creativity, thoughts, and discoveries. It's a time to become the real and greatest *you*.

> Our ordinary "I" thirsts for continuity. Our mind is never still. We dare not remain without thinking, without doing something, face to face with emptiness—a terrifying solitude. We are afraid to be alone because we are afraid *not to be, not to experience*. I experience solitude not because something is missing but because there is everything—everything is here.[15]
> —David R. Hawkins

As shown in these quotes and throughout the book, the genius in you will come during these times of drifting, in times of solitude and usually in nature. It won't come to you when you are constantly *doing*, or in the boardroom with a room full of executives. It is the form of drifting that is necessary for all of us.

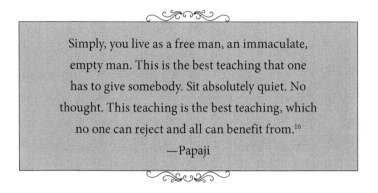

Simply, you live as a free man, an immaculate, empty man. This is the best teaching that one has to give somebody. Sit absolutely quiet. No thought. This teaching is the best teaching, which no one can reject and all can benefit from.[16]

—Papaji

Unfortunately, we have grown up in a culture that embraces busyness as a sign of success, as a necessity. We see people dressed in business suits and business attire who are on their cell phones, Blackberries, laptops, all appearing to be extremely busy, and we have the perception that this is a sign of success. And there is a good chance they *are* successful in business, but are they truly successful? If you could ask them if what they are doing now is their lifelong goal, their ultimate dream—Are they happy and free? Are they excited to go to work every day?—most would probably tell you no. Despite all outward appearances of success, there is likely a longing in most of them for something different, something greater, something better, something that moves them. And yet they, too, drift on.

In his book *Being in Balance*, Dr. Wayne Dyer writes that, "When you live your life *going through the motions*, it may seem to be convenient, but the weight of your dissatisfaction creates a huge imbalance in the only life you have now. You're perplexed by the ever-present gnawing feeling of dissatisfaction that you can't seem to shake, that pit-of-the-stomach sensation of emptiness. It shows up when you're sound asleep and your dreams are filled with reminders of what you'd love to be, but you wake and return to pursuing your safe routine."[17]

Technology has made our life much easier and more efficient, but as we are now more and more connected at all times, every spare moment we have is spent texting, checking e-mail, Facebook, Twitter, surfing the Web, leaving little time to be quiet, still, alone with our thoughts. You have to wonder how enlightened monks and sages would actually be if while they were meditating they were receiving and sending text messages and Tweets.

Many "successful" people (perhaps most of them) live in a world dominated by a giant to-do list, and it fills up relentlessly no matter how many items they scratch out. There is a constant feeling of low-level anxiety, a feeling that there is always too much to do and not enough time to do it. Henry David Thoreau was remarkably accurate when he observed that most people lead lives of quiet desperation and go to the grave with their song still with them.[18]
—Srikumar Rao

Great works of art, literature, poetry, music, business ideas, inventions—none of these came while these people were on their Blackberries, iPhones, or iPads. Perhaps fortunately for many of these people and for us, iPads and Blackberries were not invented when they came up with their masterpieces. Would Newton have ever discovered gravity while under the apple tree if he had been on his cell phone? When the apple hit him in the head while he was on his cell phone, he would have probably just been annoyed that the apple hit him and told whoever he was talking to about getting hit by an apple—and we might have been denied his wonderful discoveries. What if Leonardo da Vinci had been consumed by Facebook or cell phones? Or Michelangelo? Or Benjamin Franklin? Would we ever have been fortunate enough to witness their great works of art and inventions?

My thoughts never stop. When one has passed, another one is here, followed by another. I am attached to all of them. But if for a moment a space appears in the thinking, then there is nothing for me to be attached to. I am free. In the silence, the mind can be conscious of each movement of the thinking. The perception is free from reaction, and the energy that results is not mechanical, not the product of thought. It is the energy that spiritual seekers have been looking for throughout the ages.[19]

—Jeanne de Salzman

If you feel that any of this resonates with you, that your days are filled with a giant to-do list, that you never take any time for yourself, that you are continually *doing* all day long, then I suggest that you try drifting a little. It doesn't have to be anything drastic like quitting your job and sitting on a park bench for two years like Eckhart Tolle—even though that worked for him.

Then again, maybe you *do* need to sit on a park bench for a couple years—or a beach, a retreat in the mountains, whatever you do to get away. Only you will know. You can still be busy with your job and all of your activities, but take some time for yourself. Spend some time alone. Don't be afraid to be by yourself. I would also recommend meditation if you are able to meditate. Many people find it difficult to actually sit and do nothing. It's not easy to sit for any length of time watching your thoughts and breath with nothing to do. If you can start with short meditation sessions (five minutes) and slowly increase the time, that will help you adjust.

But you don't have to meditate. Being alone in nature, I believe, is just as effective. Running, walking, or sitting are great ways to experience time alone as well. The key is to do it daily if you can— even if it's for ten minutes in the morning or ten minutes in the evening, or both. Let the inspiration come to you in these quiet moments, because it certainly won't come to you when you're texting or checking e-mails.

> People accomplish great things through quiet moments, imagining that the invisible things from the foundation of time are clearly visible. In Greenwich Village, I met a poet who wrote beautiful poems; he had them printed on cards, and sold them at Christmastime. He said that when he got still, the words would come into his mind accompanied by a lovely scene. The Great Musician is within.[20]
> —Eckhart Tolle

I will close this section with an excerpt from *Creativity Revealed* by Scott Jeffrey:

> We must rise above the drive of the ego to control every moment and lock us into an automaton-like state. Transcending this conditioning can help us produce works of ingenuity and originality...

The "busyness syndrome," which we're all too familiar with, is a consequence of what some traditions call "Monkey Mind." Imaginary thoughts jumping from place to place, like a monkey swinging through the trees. Many of us live in Monkey Mind...

Living in Monkey Mind, most of society shuts off its creative potential, slipping into a coma-like state suited for mindlessly watching television. Living in this state, a human being blocks the Light and therefore lacks ingenuity and inventiveness.[21]

Are you living in Monkey Mind? Has it taken you anyplace great? Is it time to get out of Monkey Mind and the coma-like life you're living and tap into the universal intelligence that is available to all (in abundance) and yet used by so few? Isn't it time to take a little break from all the *doing* and let your true greatness have a chance to unfold? Maybe we are descendants of the apes, but we don't have to live like apes in zoos—unless, of course, we have allowed our Monkey Mind to put us there. Get out of the cage now and free yourself to your true potential. Let your genius emerge.

Or Not to Drift?

2

The way to start doing something is to
simply start doing something.
—Vernon Howard

After reading about all the benefits of drifting, you may be a little confused, but this book is about incorporating both inaction and action (drifting and not drifting) into your life. By *not drifting*, I mean taking action. And by taking action, I mean taking action in your life to do something different—to stop the drifting, or maybe taking action to drift. Whatever action you take, the key is doing *something*. Something different, because you know that what you are currently doing is not working.

Let's say you took the advice from the last chapter, drifted more than you ever have, and a revelation came to you. The revelation doesn't have to be something that has never been invented before. It could be an idea for a book, an aspiration to be a dancer, perhaps a determination to chase your dream of being a professional athlete. It might mean taking your dream vacation, or becoming a writer or a musician. It could be the next big idea for a business, an invention, a painting. Whatever it is that got you excited, that got your adrenaline pumping, that made you excited about life again, it's still just an idea. You can talk about it all you want, to your friends, family, or whoever will listen, but until you do something, it is only an idea.

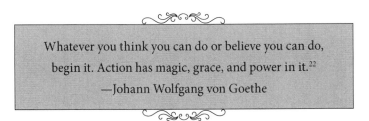

> Whatever you think you can do or believe you can do, begin it. Action has magic, grace, and power in it.[22]
> —Johann Wolfgang von Goethe

Now is when the "or not to drift" comes into play. It's time to take action and go after your dreams. This is when I would go to the monk who had been meditating in the cave for several years and tell him to come out of the cave and share his wisdom and insight with the rest of the world. You have what you feel is the greatest idea since bottled water, but until you take action, it will be buried in the eternal tomb that is home to an infinite number of great ideas that are all too soon forgotten. How many inventions, scientific theories, businesses, paintings, books, athletes are buried in this tomb? Just think of all the potential wealth that exists there! How many times have you heard your friends and family tell you about an idea for a new product that is badly needed, but that's the last time you ever hear about it? Yeah, it was a great idea, but that's all it was: an idea. Another idea come and gone. Off to the tomb.

Your soul knows when you are living in conflict (in body or mind) and are not pursuing your higher good. Your soul will do something, (eventually anything) to wake you up and get you back "on track." It usually starts with soft, gentle whispers, "Psst... wake up, Dear One. It's time to alter or release the bad dream you've been having (or living) and wake-up to A New Life." Of course if that doesn't work, the soul may say, "Hey You! Get up and move your ass, and don't look back!"[23]

—Michael Mirdad

Basically, everything that you see was at one time just an idea, a thought, nothing more. Cars, planes, shoes, paintings, businesses, sculptures, pencils, chairs, iPhones, iPads, the wheel, books—just an idea in someone's mind, until they took action. The hardest and toughest question you have is knowing when to take action. How do you know your idea has merit and it's not just another crazy dream? How do you know when to change jobs, get a job, move to a new city or live in the country, go back to college, or get your high-school diploma? How do you know? Unfortunately, I don't have a magical answer for you, but I can tell you about my experience with taking action.

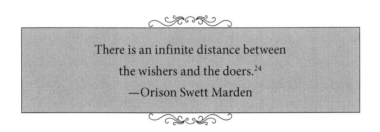

There is an infinite distance between
the wishers and the doers.[24]
—Orison Swett Marden

As you will read in chapter 3, "My Story/My Drifting," when I had my big idea, my eureka moment, my life calling, my epiphany, or whatever you might call it—if I had done nothing, had not taken action, well, who knows what I might be doing now? I hate to even entertain the thought. Maybe I would be a poor and starving writer!

You have to ask yourself, is it time to stop drifting and take action? Is it time to make your idea a reality? Do you want to go for it and see what happens, or do you want to be like one of those who Henry David Thoreau says "go to the grave with the song still in them?"[25] As I mentioned previously, you may be perfectly content and happy with your life, your accomplishments, and your career, which is great! But if there is something inside you that is telling you that you don't want to go to your grave with your song still in you, that you have much more that you want to bring out, then the concepts and ideas in this book will help you.

Only you know if your life is just a half or a quarter of what it should or could be. In his book *He Can Who Thinks He Can*, Orison Swett Marden quotes author and clergyman Phillips Brooks as saying, "No man can live a half-life when he has genuinely learned that it is a half-life."[26] Is your life a half-life? Do you still have your song in you? Are you tired of your same old routine? Living life like it was one big yesterday? If you answer even a partial yes to any of these questions, it may be time for you to take action. Time to change what you are currently doing, take the plunge, and go for it. You might be amazed at all the doors that will open for you.

In the introduction to this book, I mentioned a quote from the Greek philosopher Heraclitus: "Every walking animal is driven to its purpose with a whack."[27] Are you ready for your whack? Are you ready to be driven to a greater purpose? Are you ready to find your true calling—what you were meant to be and do? Although the previous chapter talked about the need for drifting, the need to back off, the need to slow down, to be still and open your mind to the universal intelligence, there comes a point where if you ever want to bring about your greatest aspirations, you have to take action.

Newton would just be a man getting hit by an apple if he had not developed his theory of gravity from the event. His mind was still and open to ideas at the time when his revelation came to him, but he did not continue to drift under the apple tree. He took action. He understood our inherent need to drift and our inherent need to express something greater in ourselves by taking action. It's inherent in all of us, not just Newton.

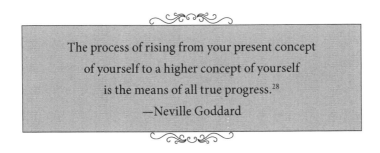

The process of rising from your present concept
of yourself to a higher concept of yourself
is the means of all true progress.[28]
—Neville Goddard

There is a time and place for taking action, and only you will know. There will be something in your gut that keeps gnawing at you, and the more you try to ignore it, the more it grows. It's like writing this book: it gnaws at me every day that I don't write. Don't ignore that feeling. It's telling you something.

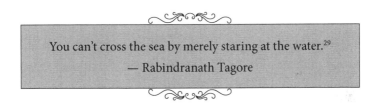

You can't cross the sea by merely staring at the water.[29]
— Rabindranath Tagore

Aren't you tired of staring at the sea? Running to the mailbox every day to see if there is something new and exciting in the mail that is going to change your life? Putting your dream off until tomorrow? And then tomorrow and then tomorrow... but tomorrow never comes.

I am not telling you to quit your job and drop everything. When I started the business I own now, I continued to work at various odd jobs. They weren't glamorous jobs. I had an engineering degree, and I was getting minimum wage on the other end of a shovel putting in a pipeline and also putting treadmills together on an assembly line. Nothing wrong with these jobs, but it certainly wasn't my life calling. I also wasn't crazy enough to put all my eggs in one basket. I would not have survived without these jobs (and my wife working as well).

Even though I worked hard at all these various jobs, my heart and soul were a million miles away dwelling on what would become TR Toppers, the business I currently own and run with my two brothers. The other jobs were just a way for me to get my dream off the ground. The various odd jobs I had were tolerable because I knew that they were only temporary, that I wouldn't be there until retirement. I didn't care that I was in my mid-thirties with a college degree working labor jobs, because I had a dream. I had something greater in me that I wanted to express. And I knew I had to take action. At the time, I hadn't read any of the books I'm quoting here, but I knew it was time to pursue my dream. As you will read, I just started chopping, one box at a time.

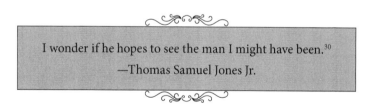

I wonder if he hopes to see the man I might have been.[30]
—Thomas Samuel Jones Jr.

I want to emphasize again that it's not an all-or-nothing deal, when and if you do take action. You will still need your drifting periods, your time alone to get away. I strongly encourage it on a daily basis.

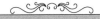

There is a bird that lives deep in the snowy mountain. Tortured by night's numbing cold, it cries that it will build a warm nest in the morning. Yet, when day breaks, it sleeps the day away, basking in the warmth of the sun. So it continues crying vainly throughout its life. People are often the same, lamenting their circumstances yet passing by every opportunity to change.[31]
—Taro Gold

Most of us tend to live like this bird. We torture ourselves on a daily basis because we know we are putting off what lies deep within us. The section of chapter 11 entitled "Don't Be the 'Usual You'" addresses just this problem. It's too easy to be the "usual you." If you don't know what your "usual you" is, then you should probably go to that section now. Most of you, however, probably know the "usual you" that I am talking about.

It is hard to change. It's hard to change the things we do day in and day out, month to month, year to year. But the good news is: you *can* change.

"If things would only change!" you cry. What is it that changes things? Wishing, or hustling?—dreaming, or working? Can you expect them to change while you merely sit down and wish them to change? How long would it take you to build a house sitting on the foundation and wishing it would go up? Wishing does not amount to anything unless it is backed up by endeavor, determination, and grit.[32]
—Orison Swett Marden

Is it time for you to take action? Or is it a time to drift? Only you can make that decision, but most likely you have a good idea which direction you need to go.

There comes an hour of sadness with the
setting of the sun, not for the sins committed
but for the things I have not done.[33]
—Minot Judson Savage

This is your big moment. This moment is eternity. *Now* is the time to make something of your life. To be proud of *yourself*, not someone else. To free *yourself*. To be what *you* can be. I don't care what age you are—it doesn't matter. People use age as an excuse. Too young, too old, too whatever… and I might throw in, maybe, too scared. Whatever your excuse is, forget it. Why not during this lifetime be great? Why wait until the next one?

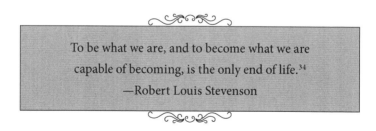

To be what we are, and to become what we are
capable of becoming, is the only end of life.[34]
—Robert Louis Stevenson

3

My Story/My Drifting

Your life story would not make a good book. Don't even try.[35]
—Fran Lebowitz

As Fran Lebowitz suggests, my life story would not make a good book. As a matter of fact, It's not a story at all. The stories in my life that I write about are just a collection of things that happened at different moments in my life. But not *a* story. A good story typically has a beginning and some type of plot. As you will find in the pages that follow, I never had a plot. I was purposeful at times and at other times without purpose—random and spontaneous, but no story. So why do I use "story" in the title of this chapter? Because it is a word that we are all familiar with. I opted for simplicity.

Life is a handful of short stories, pretending to be a novel.[36]
—Unknown

The purpose of this section of the book is to shed light on how it came about, to give you some background on my business ventures and being an entrepreneur, to tell you about the *drifting* periods of my life and the *not drifting* periods, and ultimately to share how my pursuit of freedom has been the real story of my life. Pursuing freedom has led to everything I have today, and not just material possessions. I have made freedom the passion of my life, but for most of my life, I didn't know it.

Pursuing freedom led me to the concepts and teachings that are in this book—teachings that I practice daily. A lifelong freedom quest led to the business I started twenty years ago and still currently own with my two brothers. If I had any kind of story, it would be a story of freedom. And it has always led to something better.

If there is anything in the world a person should fight for, it is freedom to pursue his ideal, because in that is his great opportunity for self-expression, for the unfoldment of the greatest thing possible to him. It is his great chance to make his life tell in the largest, completest way; to do the most original, distinctive thing possible for him.[37]
—Orison Swett Marden

As I have mentioned, I have had far more drifting in my life than times of taking action. There were and still are times when

I am lazy, content, satisfied. Why? Maybe it's necessary. Maybe I need to drift. But I do take action occasionally. I do put to use the powers and laws that are the central theme of this book. Not only the powers, but also the freedoms that come from using these laws and powers. My biggest problem? For a long time, I did not know that these powers and laws existed. I was ignorant of the powers that are available to all of us.

Despite my ignorance, I still used them on occasion. And those times that I unknowingly did use them produced the greatest things in my life. I just didn't know why. As the saying goes, "Ignorance of the law is no excuse." I was ignorant, but fortunately I bumbled and stumbled my way into using them once in a while. I believe it's innate in all of us to do so. Whether we know about these powers or not, we still have access to them. Our need for self-expansion, self-expression, and growth, regardless of our ignorance, allows us to unknowingly use these universal laws.

But if you know of these laws—universal intelligence, God, spirit, the source, infinite intelligence, or whatever you want to call it—and use them knowingly each and every day, each and every moment, your life will change dramatically. It won't be as random, with good things happening occasionally and bad things happening more often. You will no longer think of what happens to you as being "lucky" or "fortunate" or "in the right place at the right time." When you knowingly use these powers, you will know why you are lucky. And you will also know why things may have gone wrong, why perceived "bad things" always seem to happen to you.

> The mental force that controls the universe may be called anything you like and visualized any way you choose. The important thing is to understand that it exists, to know something about how it works, and what your relationship to it is. If we give just the slightest reflection to our own lives, we cannot help but be startled by how we seem dogged by the same situation in all things, year after year, time after time. This deadly recurrence is the source of most frustration and mental illness, is the bottom root of all failure.[38]
>
> —U. S. Andersen

I only wish that I had been exposed to the ideas and concepts in this book much earlier in my life. These are laws and powers that have been taught throughout the ages by all the great spiritual teachers, sages, and prophets—universal laws that have been used by and professed by Jesus, the Buddha, and countless other prophets and enlightened beings. My journey has been a slow process over many years of coming out of my personal darkness. And by *darkness*, I don't mean a long period of depression. My life has been a long, slow awakening to the light revealed in this book. What follows are specific periods, moments, events, and "stories" that I feel are relevant to this book. I will show you how I occasionally and unknowingly used these powers.

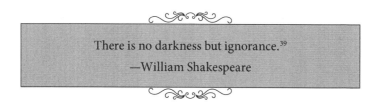

> There is no darkness but ignorance.[39]
>
> —William Shakespeare

I also don't want you to think as I write about some of my experiences in my life that I am tooting my own horn. Nothing I have done is special. When I write about starting my own business, I know that millions of others have done exactly the same thing—not the same business, but the principle behind starting any business is basically the same. I want to show that most of my life has been centered around not doing the "usual," not following the crowd. What it boils down to is my personal freedom. I had to have it.

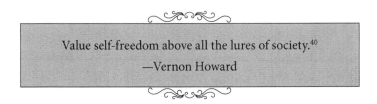

Value self-freedom above all the lures of society.[40]

—Vernon Howard

THE EARLY YEARS

You have to do your own growing, no matter
how tall your grandfather was.[41]
—Abraham Lincoln

I think of my years through high school primarily as drifting years. Basically, I was spoon-fed life by other people. Almost everything I learned about life came from my parents, teachers, friends, other family members, doctors, church, counselors—mostly people in positions of authority who I looked up to (literally). Not too many original thoughts of my own. I am not saying this was good or bad; it's just the way it was. I think it's true for most of us. During this time, we don't yet know a lot about the world or life, so we rely on people we respect to tell us about it. During this time, we establish most of our beliefs about life, and for many of us, these ideas and beliefs stay with us for a lifetime.

I will give you an example of this. Ask any child what religion or religious denomination he or she belongs to, and most would tell you Christian, Catholic, Baptist, Lutheran, or Jewish (at least in the United States). And why or how did they choose this particular religion or denomination? In most cases, they didn't. They went to church with their parents, and that's the church their parents were raised in, and their parents, and their parents. I did the same thing. My mother took us to the Lutheran church. If someone asked me what denomination or religion I belonged to, I would tell them Lutheran. And I always felt proud to tell them. I didn't choose that particular denomination, but I trusted that my mother knew what she was doing.

My point is not to single out religion, but to show that almost everything I learned and accepted about life as being true or right came from other people. I accepted it, and it became true for me. If my mom had been Hindu, I would have been Hindu. Catholic, I would have been Catholic. Buddhist, I would have been Buddhist. It's the way most of us were raised. We trusted our parents and our elders, and we believed what they told us.

One thing that stands out about religion and going to church during this time of my life, and a thing that really troubled me, was that if you didn't accept Jesus as your savior and repent of your sins, your chances of getting into heaven were not good. Not only not good, it most likely wouldn't happen. Since this message came from my Sunday School teacher—again, someone I looked up to and respected—I accepted it as gospel. What bothered me was the knowledge that my father didn't go to church. Did this mean he wouldn't be with us in heaven? The family would be together in heaven, but we would be missing one key member. Our dad was one of the kindest and gentlest human beings I have ever met or been associated with, but according to what I was being taught, I was going to be in this wonderful place after I died and my father wouldn't be there. How could that be wonderful? An eternity without my father? To me, at that time in my life, that seemed more like hell.

I spent many sleepless nights worrying about death and what would happen with my family. Religion and going to church were making me lose sleep at the thought of not being with my dad in the afterlife. Despite the many good things I learned from going to church, the thought of spending an eternity without my father scared me. I wasn't concerned about myself, because I was going to church—I would be okay! But an eternity without my father?

As I look back now, I appreciate my mother exposing us to religion, and there were many great experiences that I fondly remember about going to church with my mom and brothers, but the fear and anxiety it created had a much greater influence on my life than the good I was being taught. For me, religion and the concept of heaven and hell scared me to death! That was a lot to deal with as a child. Not only as a child, but as an adult as well.

My philosophies and beliefs have changed about religion, but I still feel it is an important and necessary part of many people's lives. I am not writing to change any of your beliefs. I may not belong to a specific denomination any longer, but there is infinite wisdom and good that I take from all the world religions and spiritual teachings. Whether you are a Christian, a Jew, a Buddhist,… the fundamental teaching that seems to be overlooked and is central to most world religions is to *see* "God" in everything. See "Buddha" in everything. See "perfection" in everything and everyone. That is and should be the bottom-line of all religions. Unfortunately, we tend to have the mentality that the religion or faith that we belong to is the right one—that we just happen to be fortunate enough to be the chosen ones, lucky enough to have been born into the right religion. Thus, the cause of most of the world's conflicts and suffering.

The early years are our impressionable years. We are new to the world, and we want people to tell us about it. There is no shortage of people willing to do that. We are given lots of opinions, lots of advice, lots of what-to-do, lots of what-not-to-do—everyone has an opinion on what's good for us.

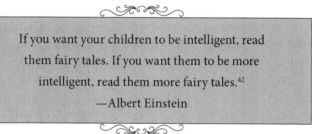

If you want your children to be intelligent, read them fairy tales. If you want them to be more intelligent, read them more fairy tales.[42]
—Albert Einstein

MY HOMETOWN

Your hometown is where they can't figure out
how you did as well as you did.[43]
—Unknown

I grew up in a small ranching town in Eastern Oregon called Baker City (just "Baker" when I was growing up). Baker City is nestled in a valley next to the Elkhorn mountain range. If you have never been to Eastern Oregon or Baker City, it is one of the most scenic towns in the country—with valleys, pristine lakes and rivers, the Eagle Cap mountains, snowcapped peaks, and an abundance of pine trees. It is an outdoorsman's paradise. If you want to see real-life cowboys or cowgirls, you will find them in Baker City. It's a historic town, much like you would envision in the old Western days: ranching, cattle, horses, logging, bars, saloons. The stuff the Wild West was famous for was just a way of life in Baker City and still is.

My life in Baker during this time consisted of school, playing sports, hunting, hiking, and camping. I fully embraced everything Eastern Oregon had to offer. I loved growing up in Baker. When I wasn't going to school or playing sports, I was chukar hunting on the Snake River. A chukar is a game bird that is smaller than a pheasant and larger than a quail, and it thrives on the hilly terrain and canyons of the Snake River (forty minutes from Baker). On the weekends during hunting season, I was on the Snake River with my father, brothers, or friends. We also had skiing within thirty minutes at a little ski area called Anthony Lakes.

And I played golf. Lots and lots of golf. Baker at that time had a nine-hole golf course that I played at least a million rounds on (maybe exaggerating a little). During the spring and summer when I wasn't working, I was on the golf course. For me, Baker was the perfect place to grow up. It was my personal paradise, my personal heaven.

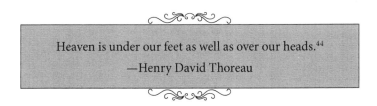

Heaven is under our feet as well as over our heads.[44]
—Henry David Thoreau

My father owned a meat-packing plant in Baker with his brother and father, the Eastern Oregon Meat Company. My brothers and I grew up working at the meat company, and our father instilled a good work ethic in us, or at least tried to. I also believe my two brothers and I got our entrepreneurial spirit from our dad. He had us selling night crawlers (worms for fishing) at an early age—our first experience of being entrepreneurs! He would get up at five every morning to go to work at the meat company, and he would not come home until after six in the evening. And then he would take us out at dark to hunt for night crawlers during the summer. I am more impressed that he would do this after working ten to twelve hours at the meat company than the fact that we were getting our first taste of entrepreneurship.

We sold the night crawlers for twenty-five cents a dozen, so we certainly weren't going to get rich. We had to catch a lot of night crawlers to make any money, especially once it was split three ways. But the entrepreneurial seed had been planted.

I was fortunate to be raised in a family in which our lives revolved around some type of work. Whether it was the family business at the meat company, selling night crawlers, selling manure for fertilizer, working for someone else—our father loved work and instilled it in us. I personally never loved work, especially shoveling and selling manure or catching night crawlers!

It was never really about the money for my father. It was the fact that we were working. He never emphasized the money factor. It was just understood that if you worked hard, the money would come.

The thing I do remember my dad telling me about working for someone else was that they pay you their money to do a job, and no matter how menial the job may be, you give them your best effort and work hard. The amount they were paying you was not related to the effort. You worked hard regardless of the pay.

That thought was always in the back of my mind no matter who I was working for.

Our little business ventures had a lasting impression on us, and I thank my father for that. Even at our young age, there was freedom that came from being in business for ourselves. The more night crawlers we would catch at night, the more money we would make. The more manure we would shovel and sell, the more money we would make. We were learning, without really knowing it, that we could create our future—that we reap what we sow.

I haven't mentioned much about our mother, but she too had a big influence on our lives and supported everything we did, including school, sports, and work. She was responsible for getting us into golf, which we are all eternally grateful for! She also exposed us to things in life that are not typical, especially for boys in a Western cowboy town—like music, the arts, literature, and good grammar. Thankfully, our mother and father were different in good ways. It was going to be our job to take the good from both.

There are many other things I could write about growing up in Baker. I could fill up the rest of the book, but very little would be of interest to you. Nothing stands out that would be significant, with the exception of being raised by wonderful parents who encouraged us to do whatever we wanted. I consider myself extremely lucky. I treasure this time of my life and wouldn't trade it for anything. I can't Imagine (at least for me) a better place to grow up than Eastern Oregon. I loved it.

THE COLLEGE YEARS

College is a refuge from hasty judgment.[45]
—Robert Frost

After high school, I ventured off to college without giving it a whole lot of thought. In our family, it was just assumed that going to college was what you did after high school. Not that we were wealthy by any stretch of the imagination, but we (my brothers and I) took it for granted that college was the next step. That's why we worked during the summer and also during school—to help pay for college. I'm sure it came from our parents, although I never remember a time when they specifically said that we *had* to go to college. They encouraged us, but it was never mandatory.

I certainly had no clue what I wanted to do with my life. I needed college if for no other reason than to collect my thoughts on life and what I might do with it. If nothing else, college teaches you—if you want to graduate, that is—to show up, listen, and try to learn, and to do the best you can, even while on your own for the first time. You have no one pushing you but *you*. It's the first time in your life when you know you need to "get it done" or you will be packing your bags.

The one thing I knew for sure in college was I liked my personal freedom and I wanted to be wealthy. I didn't know how or what field to go into, but I knew I wanted freedom and money. My father used to ask me what I was interested in doing, and I would tell him that I didn't know, but I was going to be rich. That answer drove him crazy. You have to understand that my father was a "man's man." I can't define exactly what that is, but whatever it is—that's what he was. He grew up working. He loved to work, and he would work ten or twelve hours a day without giving it a second thought. That's what he did. So for me to make a comment like this was not only obnoxious but laughable to him. His standard reply to my remark was always, "You're a dreamer." And I would have to agree with him. I'm glad that I was.

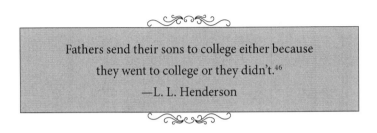

Fathers send their sons to college either because they went to college or they didn't.[46]
—L. L. Henderson

I chose to go to Oregon State University in Corvallis, Oregon. I'm still not sure why, except that it was a well-known, respected university and it was in Oregon (in-state tuition). Both of my brothers went to the University of Oregon in Eugene, so someone had to be a rebel. I had no plan when I went to college—no idea of what I wanted to do or study. I started in business and after a year changed to engineering. The main reason for the change was that I liked the math and physics in engineering, and even though I could not set a mousetrap, I was going to be an engineer. I knew absolutely nothing about engineering or what engineers actually did. In practical terms, I was a disgrace to the engineering profession. I had no interest in how things worked, and I didn't know what a Phillips-head screwdriver was until I was out of college. The only thing I could "fix" was lunch. But book-wise, I did okay.

College tends to steer you in a specific career direction, whether from your own aspirations, your parents', or your counselor's, which is great for people who know what they want to do. But the only thing I knew at that time in my life was that I wanted to be rich. Unfortunately, I didn't see "getting rich" on the college curriculum, with the exception maybe of becoming a doctor (and I had no interest in the field of medicine). I chose engineering mainly because the classes were more interesting to me than other fields. I also had business as a minor because deep down I must have known that the entrepreneurial seed that had been planted when I was much younger would always be a part of me.

The business classes were helpful, but there were no courses offered on becoming an entrepreneur, no classes on someday owning your own business and the risks and rewards associated with being self-employed. I hope this has changed over the years, but the bottom line was that I was going to get my degree in engineering because you had to declare some type of major. And ultimately, that was why I was attending college—to get a degree.

It's great to learn everything you can, but you can also do that without going to college. College, to me, was all about getting the college degree. Once I had my degree, then I could pursue my dream of becoming rich.

The first couple years at Oregon State were drifting years. I joined a fraternity, did fine in school, had lots of freedoms, but there was something missing in my life. I felt adrift, just going through the motions to get my degree. As I mentioned, I didn't really know what engineers did for sure, but it never seemed overly interesting to me. I am in no way putting down engineering, as it is a worthy and admirable profession. Personally, however, I was not enthralled by it—but I trudged onward in the pursuit of a degree. It was all about the degree. I was drifting, but I didn't know it.

PLANTING SEEDS

All my life I have tried to pluck a thistle and plant a flower
wherever the thought would grow in thought and mind.[47]

—Abraham Lincoln

The experience I am going to share is my first life-changing use
of the universal laws available to all of us. I planted the seed. Even
though I didn't know anything about planting seeds or using
universal powers, I did some planting.

Planting seeds is just how it sounds. You plant a seed of corn,
water and fertilize it, take care of it, and you will soon have corn.
From the seed to the corn; from the acorn to the oak tree. The
same principle applies to carrots, flowers, radishes—in fact, all
of nature, including humans, has access to this universal power.
Humans are a little different in that we plant the seeds in our
minds. Most of the time we don't realize that we do this or that
we even have this power to "grow" anything we want to "harvest"
(good or bad).

Without going into too much detail on planting seeds, a
topic that has been central to the teachings of enlightened beings
throughout the ages, I will give you a few examples of how people
use this power, knowingly or unknowingly, on a daily basis. Let's
say a thought pops into your head that it's time to buy a new
car. The new car seed has now been planted. You may mention
it to your spouse, family, or whoever, and the next thing you
know you are at the car dealer looking at cars. You like the Jeep
Grand Cherokee, and now everywhere you look when you are
driving, you see Jeep Grand Cherokees. They're everywhere! After
researching, going from car lot to car lot, talking to salesmen,
lo and behold, you find yourself driving your new Jeep Grand

Cherokee. All from a thought. The new car seed that you planted allowed you to reap the harvest of a new Jeep Grand Cherokee.

> The subconscious mind will accept your beliefs and your convictions. It is like the soil; it will accept any seed that you deposit in it, whether it is good or bad. Remember: Anything that you accept as true and believe in will be accepted by your subconscious mind, and brought into your life as a condition, experience, or event.[48]
> —Joseph Murphy

This planting applies to almost everything we do. You see a brochure on the Hawaiian Islands and think how nice it would be to take the family or just yourself on a vacation and relax on the beach in Hawaii for a few days. Whether you can afford the vacation or not, you look into airfare, check out hotels, call travel agents, and surf the Web for deals. You are watering your vacation seed and watching it grow. Finally, after much tender loving care, lots of watering and fertilizing, you're in Hawaii sipping a piña colada in a cabana under a palm tree. You planted the vacation seed, and the next thing you know you're on vacation.

Maybe, instead, you're going to the movies after planting the movie seed. Or watching TV. Or reading a book. Or deciding to order a pizza. Taking up tennis. Becoming an artist. Taking piano lessons. All just a seed of thought that turns into whatever you planted. We reap and sow every day.

This all seems simple and mundane, but most of us don't think about or know that we are doing this. We don't know what seeds we are planting or why. We also don't know the real power behind our planting. You can plant small seeds, like going to the grocery store, or large ones, like building a new home or starting a new career. I will give examples of times that I planted what I consider to be major seeds in my life and how they have come to fruition—all from a thought. But you also have to be careful about the seeds you plant, because just as in nature, flowers can grow right next to weeds. Weeds will flourish if nurtured and taken care of. Our job is to only water and nurture the good seeds.

In their 1996 song "Bleeding Me,"[49] the heavy-metal band Metallica sang about being tormented by a thorn that came from a tree they planted. The songwriters understood that the pain we experience in life is from negative seeds that we ourselves plant. We all plant negative seeds, and we also tend to focus more on the negative seeds than the positive seeds. To give you an example, you might plant seeds about something you don't like about your body, your face, your coworkers, your lack of money, your poor health— and the more you focus and dwell on this negative planting, the more you nourish and grow the negative seed. Pretty soon this small, seemingly harmless thought or seed has blossomed into a full-grown weed, or as in Metallica's case, a tree of thorns. It may grow wildly and out of control if you focus and dwell on it every day.

The more you focus on that bad seed, the more you make it a part of your life, the more it will consume your life. By watering the negative seeds, you will sprout new branches of thorns, and pretty soon you will be consumed by a plant or tree that is covered with thorns and has the potential to affect every aspect of your life. So we need to be very careful about the seeds that we plant, and even more careful about the ones we water and give our attention to.

One thing to remember when you do plant seeds is that it is fine to water and nurture them, but just as in nature, you can't make corn grow any faster. Nature will do its part in due time, just as it will for you. Trying to help anything grow faster doesn't work. So let nature do its job and expect to harvest what you plant with unwavering conviction. Now, with this background in mind, I'll tell you about my first major planting in my life.

THE BIG MOVE

An ant on the move does more than a dozing ox.[50]

—Lao Tzu

I was in my second year at Oregon State. It was another rainy, dreary, cold January day in Corvallis, Oregon, and I was watching a college tennis match on TV in the basement of our fraternity. If you have heard stories about the rain in Western Oregon, they're all true. The clouds roll in sometime in late October or early November, hover fifty feet above your head with a slow steady drizzle of rain, and then occasionally lift sometime in March. There's a reason Western Oregon is green. The best part about the rain, besides the greenery and vegetation, is your new appreciation for the sun when it does finally peek out! There's beauty when something is taken away from you and then finally given back. At this point, though, after what seemed like the fiftieth straight day of rain, I was a little down in the dumps, depressed by the weather and tired of drifting. I needed a change. I needed something different in my life.

As I was watching this college tennis match on TV, what stood out most was the blue sky, palm trees, students in shorts and

T-shirts, and most importantly, the fact that it was *live*. It wasn't recorded—it was being played at that moment. Somewhere, in the middle of January, there was sunshine, palm trees, and warm weather. Where could this mirage be?

The match was being played at Arizona State University in Tempe. I sat there in awe. The rain and dreariness were beginning to take a toll on me, and mild depression was setting in. A college campus with sunshine, palm trees, shorts and T-shirts seemed like the perfect answer to my increasingly depressed state. I made up my mind that day, that moment, that I was going to school at Arizona State. I didn't know how, but it was going to happen. It had to happen. I planted the seed.

My family couldn't afford to send me to an out-of-state school, but I was going anyway. Somehow, some way, I was leaving the rain for the sunshine. From a Beaver to a Sun Devil—it was going to happen. I planted the seed, and I was going to water and nurture it.

I took a semester off school to work and help pay for the out-of-state tuition. Everyone told me I was crazy. I didn't know anyone. I couldn't afford it. But none of that stopped me. And the following year, I loaded up my Chrysler Newport that my grandfather had given me and headed south for Arizona. I was going to reap what I had sown. I was going to be a Sun Devil. I was leaving the rain and cold for sunshine and palm trees. A year earlier, it was just a thought on a cold, dreary day in Western Oregon, and now it was becoming a reality. All from a thought. All from planting a seed and then watering and nurturing the seed I had planted. I was using universal powers and I didn't know it. But I was reaping the rewards.

It turned out to be one of the best moves of my life. I didn't know a soul at ASU, but there was an overwhelming feeling of freedom as I drove through the vast wide-open spaces of Nevada on my way to Arizona. I had never felt that free in my life. Even though I didn't have reverse gear in my Chrysler, I didn't have a care—I just had to be careful where I parked. I was off in pursuit of freedom. I was now a student at Arizona State. I was a Sun Devil.

Because of my love for golf, I ended up caddying at Paradise Valley Country Club in Phoenix to help pay for school. I was caddying at one of the nicest country clubs in Phoenix, getting paid, and I could play golf there after four every day for free! Not only was I making money for school, but I could play golf on one of the premier courses in the area. I was in heaven.

Just when I thought it couldn't get any better, one Saturday morning I was caddying for a gentleman who was on the board for the Evans Golf Scholarship Foundation for caddies. To make a long story short, I was offered the Evans scholarship, and it paid for my tuition and books. Picture *Caddyshack*! I was getting paid to walk around a beautiful golf course, I could play golf for free, and now I was going to get my school paid for. A year earlier, I had been slowly sinking into a state of depression from school, the rain, the drifting, and now I was basking in the sun.

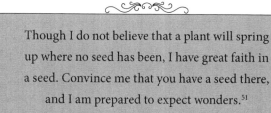

Though I do not believe that a plant will spring up where no seed has been, I have great faith in a seed. Convince me that you have a seed there, and I am prepared to expect wonders.[51]
—Henry David Thoreau

Despite not knowing what I was doing, I was now planting seeds and creating my reality. I was becoming the captain of my ship. I was making personal freedom a priority in my life. I was using universal laws. I just didn't know it.

I will share one short story about one of my engineering classes at Arizona State—yes, despite my inability to fix anything, I was still an engineering major. I was taking an engineering communication class my senior year, and for the final we had to give a speech on topics related to our specific type of engineering (electrical, mechanical, etc.). The degree I was pursuing was a little different in that it was more closely related to industrial engineering, with a minor in business. After hours and hours of listening to long, boring speeches on chemical, mechanical, and electrical engineering topics, I asked the professor if I could do my speech on the basic strategy of blackjack and how if you mastered this strategy, you could improve your odds against the casino.

To my surprise, he reluctantly said it was okay. Like I said, after listening to speech after speech on some of the most boring topics I could possibly imagine—and judging by the rest of the sleeping students, I was not alone—you can imagine their surprise when I began my speech on blackjack, the glitz and glamour of Las Vegas, and improving your odds against the casino. All of a sudden, nobody was sleeping anymore. Not exactly what anyone was expecting. But to my surprise, everyone loved the speech and asked lots of questions, and even the professor enjoyed it. Students came up to me after class to talk to me about the speech and tell me how much they liked it. I was in shock.

The reason I am telling you this story is not to boast about the speech, but to explain why at that moment in my college life, I realized I wasn't cut out to be an engineer. Engineering wasn't part of my "chemical, mechanical, or electrical" makeup. It wasn't "me." As I was writing and also giving my blackjack speech, I felt excitement about my topic. I felt passionate. And I knew the other students could feel and sense my passion and enthusiasm. I also knew that I would never have that kind of passion or enthusiasm for engineering. I knew that if I had given a speech on industrial engineering, there would be no heart and soul behind it. It would have been boring and lifeless. As you will find out, however, that didn't stop me from trying to get a job as an engineer. Still, deep down, I knew it wasn't meant to be.

A REAL JOB

No man can succeed in a line of endeavor which he does not like.[52]
—Napoleon Hill

Despite everything I have said about engineering and the fact that I knew I could not be one, I still needed money and a job. I had my bachelor of science degree in engineering from ASU and thought it would not be a problem to find a job. After all, I had put in all that time in school, I thought I was smart, and now I was toting my newly acquired college degree with me.

Was I ever wrong. I had no idea it would be that hard to get a job out of college. One of the problems was, I had a degree that no one understood what it was. An engineering degree with a business minor? What's that? What skills do you have? What experience? "Experience"? I just got out of college! Despite sending out tons of resumes, interviewing on campus, and knocking on hundreds of doors, I found that no one wanted me. Not one job offer.

When I was just about ready to trash my seemingly worthless degree, I got a call from McDonnell Douglas in Long Beach, California. They wanted to offer me a job as an "aeronautical engineer." Aeronautical engineer! Me? I had no idea what an aeronautical engineer was or what I would actually do, but I jumped at the chance to be one! It sounded good. It sounded impressive.

How airplanes can actually fly has always boggled my mind—but I could get past that. I never did and still don't understand how the increased airflow over the wings creating a pressure differential concept works, and how it enables a gigantic piece of metal to get off the ground and stay off the ground. I'm amazed every time I see a jet take off and land. And I also never wanted to know how or why. I like to travel by air, but I don't need to know how the plane flies, as long as it does. I have a difficult enough time making a paper airplane, and when I do, the chances are pretty good that it won't fly. But none of this mattered, because I was now going to be an "aeronautical engineer." And I was proud of it!

My need for money and a job at that point in my life was more important than pursuing my dream of being rich. I knew I would have time to pursue my real dream. Right then, I needed a job and cash coming in.

So I packed my bags and headed to Southern California. Beaches, sunshine, palm trees, and a job as an aeronautical engineer. Life was good—until I started work. What stood out most the first week was my conversation with an engineer who had been there for twenty years and sat across the aisle from where my desk was. Twenty years and one aisle over? He was also making roughly $20,000 more than I was. My life flashed before my eyes. Was I going to be at McDonnell Douglas twenty years from now, having moved just one or two aisles over? Hop on the 405 freeway every morning and slowly make my way to the Long Beach headquarters to be there by 7:42 a.m., work until 4:42 p.m., and then get back on the same slower 405 freeway going the other direction back home? Was this going to be my life? Knowing my future and how much I would be making in twenty years? I didn't want that. I had always dreamed of being rich and free. How was that going to happen in this scenario?

Despite my life passing before my eyes, I had no alternatives. I was engaged to be married, and I needed a job. Plus, it was only the first week—I had to give it a chance. As the weeks passed, however, it was obvious that they didn't need me. I had nothing to do. The department I was in had been allocated funds for my position, so even though they didn't need me, they didn't want to lose the allocated funds for "their" budget. This would never happen in a small business, but when you become as large as McDonnell Douglas was at that time, I guess that's what you do. You have committees, budgets, meeting after meeting—all the things that are necessary to put you out of business.

I would show up at 7:42 and leave at 4:42 and not do one thing all day! The only constructive thing I did all week was walk to the payroll office to pick up my check. And I made decent money for doing nothing. I was also bored out of my mind and slowly going crazy. As time went on, it only got worse. Imagine sitting at your desk for eight hours, no computer, no work, and a clock staring at you that moved slower than the traffic on the 405 freeway. I was going insane.

Fortunately (at least for me), McDonnell Douglas had a massive layoff of engineers, and I was "lucky" enough to be one of the engineers getting his walking papers. It only made sense, since I hadn't done one thing for six months. In this case, I got my "running papers"—I got out of there as fast as I possibly could and never looked back. I had never felt freer or happier. I had no job, I was getting married in a few months, I had no place to live, no money… and I was on cloud nine. I had my freedom back!

The English poet William Blake wrote, "I must create a system or be enslaved by another man's,"[53] and that sums up my life in one sentence. I knew after my experience with McDonnell Douglas that I would never be free unless I created my own system. I had never felt so imprisoned in my entire life as I did in my short stint in Southern California. I am certainly not blaming McDonnell Douglas, as it not only offered me a job but at one time was one of the premier aircraft companies in the world, with brilliant engineers and skilled professionals. It just wasn't for me. I actually should be grateful for the time spent there, as it made me crave freedom that much more—to be independent, to create my own reality.

I am also not implying that you have to be an entrepreneur or work for yourself to "create a system." If you find something you love to do, whether you are working for yourself or someone else, then you are creating your own system. But I had the entrepreneurial spirit, and I knew it would be my ticket for creating my own system, my own freedom.

THE ICE CREAM MAN

A great many people prefer a small certainty to a big uncertainty.[54]
—Orison Swett Marden

A young boy approaches the ice-cream truck and asks, "Is it tomorrow? My mommy said I can have an ice cream tomorrow."

When I was driving an ice-cream truck, a young boy asked me that very question. My brothers and I owned two trucks—music, popsicles, Nutty Buddies, Fudgsicles, the works—that we operated in our hometown of Baker for two years during our summer breaks from college. Yes, we were the ice-cream men. We transformed two small postal jeeps into white ice-cream trucks with our logo, Rodey's Ice Cream, plastered on the side as well as pictures of our frozen treats. A speaker on top of the truck blasted popular ice-cream jingles. The kids loved us and the parents hated us, but we were in business. We were becoming entrepreneurs.

After my short-lived career as an aeronautical engineer, I took my degree to Boise, Idaho, to become what I knew best—the ice-cream man. From aeronautical engineer to ice-cream man—that had to make my new mother-in-law proud!

My brothers and I took a handwritten statement of our two years of operating the trucks in Baker (our version of a financial statement) to the bank in Baker in hopes of getting a loan and expanding the business into Boise, Idaho. We asked for a loan to acquire thirty trucks for the Boise market. We had scribbled some handwritten projections on a legal pad of what we expected to do in Boise and presented it to the bank. Times have certainly changed, as the bank loaned us $50,000 based on those handwritten projections. We purchased thirty mail trucks from the postal service, and our little ice-cream business suddenly got bigger. We were about to get serious about being the ice-cream men.

Perhaps it was the seed that our father planted in us when we were younger, when we were selling night crawlers and manure. Selling something—that's what entrepreneurs do. Business isn't all that complicated. You find a product or service that is needed and someone who is willing to pay you for that product or service, and you're in business. The entrepreneurial seed had been planted at an early age, and now the seed was starting to blossom into our first "real" business. We were willing to do whatever it took to make the ice-cream business a reality and successful.

Getting the trucks ready for the upcoming season was no easy task, as we had to sand all thirty trucks for painting, build insulated cooler boxes for the ice-cream bars (kept frozen with dry ice), install the music systems, and put decals and menus on all the trucks. It was a major undertaking, but it never seemed like work. We were building a dream. Building our business. Building our future. We were the ice-cream men. We were creating a system.

Owning and operating thirty ice-cream trucks is not as easy as it might seem. The hardest part, besides the long hours, were employee issues and high turnover. It takes a special person to want to drive an ice-cream truck for ten to twelve hours a day. We had the usual problems that any new start-up business experiences, but the only way to do it is jump in, get your feet wet, and learn as you go.

Our typical day would start with preparing routes for the drivers (we had the city mapped into specific areas for each driver). We also had to prepare personal inventory sheets for each driver each day with a specific number of ice-cream bars. The inventories would vary based on the driver's sales history as well as the area he or she was going to that day; some areas were better than others.

When the drivers would arrive to load their ice-cream trucks in the morning, we would have to go into the freezer and personally retrieve each order. The freezer was set at minus twenty degrees and even in the summertime, minus twenty degrees is cold! Each driver would receive twelve to fifteen different varieties of ice-cream bars and popsicles. Picture thirty drivers lined up waiting to get their order for the day as we scrambled around in the freezer like madmen getting each order. It was not only cold, it was hectic and chaotic.

The drivers would sign off on their inventory sheets, and at night when they came back, the money they brought in—which was counted by us as well as each driver—was supposed to correspond to the number of bars they sold that day based on their remaining inventory. Since it was an all-cash business, let's just say it didn't always work out correctly. Any shortages were deducted from the driver's pay, a policy that wasn't popular, but it was our only control over the inventory and the money.

We had an account set up at a local gas station that was near our warehouse, and after the drivers finished loading their trucks in the morning, they would all head to the gas station to fill their trucks with gas. Seeing thirty ice-cream trucks all lined up at the gas station was quite a sight! Besides gas, mechanical repairs, and breakdowns, our other biggest expense was dry ice to keep the bars frozen. Dry ice at that time cost approximately twenty-five to thirty cents a pound, and each truck would leave with approximately thirty pounds of dry ice each day. The dry ice was cut into five-pound slabs and wrapped in newspaper to enable the drivers to handle it and move it around as they searched for their bars.

Once the trucks had all left the warehouse for the day, we would organize and clean the warehouse, run any errands that needed to be done, and head out to the golf course! We had to have a little fun. Of course, we had our trusty pagers with us in case one of the trucks broke down, which happened almost daily and oftentimes more than once a day. It was a miracle if we actually finished eighteen holes of golf. There was no worse sound than to have the pager go off in the middle of your round on the golf course.

This was in the early to mid-eighties, and unfortunately cell phones were not yet on the market—at least, not affordable ones—so when a driver would break down, he or she would either have to borrow the phone in someone's home or locate a phone booth (those tall glass objects that used to be outside of convenience stores). Not only would the drivers have to find a phone, but we too would have to end our round of golf and quickly find a phone to call the drivers and find out where they were. Cell phones would have been a godsend!

If we couldn't fix the problem over the phone, we would have to tow the truck back to the warehouse. This went on seven days a week for five to six months. The only break we got was rain and bad weather—a welcome sight at times, since it meant we got a day off.

My brothers and I had our ups and downs the first year, but overall the business was successful. We were in business for ourselves, we were young and fearless, and most importantly for me, we were free. We decided to expand into Utah, targeting the Ogden and Salt Lake City markets. We bought more trucks, and during our heyday had a fleet of fifty to sixty. Our season ran from the middle of March to the middle of September, weather permitting. The hours were long; we got the trucks ready in the mornings for the drivers to be on the road by ten a.m., and during the summer the trucks would not return until dusk or later.

Despite the long hours, employee issues, breakdowns, melting ice cream, and occasional theft of the trucks, we—my two brothers and I and our wives—had a great time. We were working for ourselves, learning the ropes of business. We were even marginally profitable. Times were good! I could fill up the rest of the book with tales from our ice-cream days—a driver taking a truck to Nevada to gamble, a driver arrested for trespassing on the property of J. R. Simplot (the Idaho potato king) and trying to sell him ice cream, wrecks, abusive calls, threats from parents to stay out of their neighborhood… just about anything else you could possibly think might happen, happened.

One of the most memorable (and worst) days was when I received a frantic call after all the trucks had left the warehouse from one of the drivers who told me there had been a terrible accident involving one of our trucks. He told me there was ice cream scattered up and down the highway, and then he hung up! I had no idea where he was or where the wreck was, and I had no way to get in touch with him. It seemed like an eternity before I was finally contacted by the state police.

As it turned out, several of the drivers were racing each other as they were heading out to their routes. One of the drivers lost control of his jeep, the jeep rolled, and the driver was thrown from the vehicle. When I arrived at the scene, ice-cream boxes and bars were everywhere, the truck was demolished, and I felt sick to my stomach. It was my worst nightmare, but it was not a dream. They had already air-lifted the driver to the hospital. I was even sicker to my stomach. Fortunately, he did eventually recover from the accident, but it was a harrowing experience, and it made for some terrifying moments and sleepless nights. And it was also something I never wanted to experience again.

We ran the business for three or four more years, but as we faced more and more competition—primarily from former employees buying their own trucks—sales were starting to dwindle, and we knew it was time to get out. Fortunately, we were able to sell the business, pay off our debts, and have a little money left to live on for a while. The good news was, we got out at the right time. The bad news was, we were now unemployed. But it was a good ride, and one that I will forever cherish.

MORE DRIFTING

After selling the ice-cream business, my brothers and I were all more or less in a drifting state, taking various jobs to keep some cash coming in until something better came along. I knew that any job I might get would not be permanent, but had no idea what I might do next. I continued to try to find an engineering job, more for security than actually wanting to be an engineer. During this time of drifting, my wife and I were in Las Vegas on vacation, and while sitting by the pool reading the *Las Vegas Review Journal*, we saw on the front page of the "Homes" section what I thought was the most beautiful home I had ever seen. It was my dream house. I had to have a house like that.

I cut the page out and told my wife that someday we were going to build this home. Keep in mind, I was in Las Vegas, sitting by the pool, no job, basically no money, no prospects for a job, and yet I knew that someday I would be living in that house. My father was right when he said, "You're a dreamer."

I planted the house seed on that sunny day in Las Vegas by the pool. I was using universal laws again, although I still didn't know it. I had no plan or means of making it a reality, but none of that stopped me from believing that one day I would build that home. I tucked the paper in my suitcase and left Las Vegas with even less money, but with a new seed planted: the house seed. The seed didn't know that I didn't have any money, that I didn't have a job, that I had no prospects for a job. It's like a seed for corn that doesn't know if it will have water and sunshine but trusts nature to do its part.

FROZEN YOGURT

After our short retirement from the ice-cream business and a few attempts to find real jobs, we saw an ad in the paper for a frozen-yogurt franchise. We knew very little about frozen yogurt, but it was the mid-eighties and frozen yogurt was the new craze on the rise. Finally there was hope to be in business for ourselves again. My brothers and I, plus another partner, looked at several yogurt franchises and decided on J Higby's Yogurt & Treat Shops. The franchise was based in Sacramento, California. J Higby's yogurt tasted like ice cream, the stores had a colorful design and an extensive topping bar, and the overall concept of J Higby's appealed to all of us. We made up our minds to get into the frozen-yogurt business, and J Higby's was the franchise we chose.

Based on our success with the ice-cream business, we were able to arrange financing for a new frozen-yogurt shop, and we opened our first official J Higby's in Ogden, Utah, in the Ogden City Mall. I was living in Ogden and now had gone from being the ice-cream man to the frozen-yogurt guy. Aeronautical engineer to ice-cream man to frozen-yogurt man! Life takes some strange twists and turns, but we were back in business after our short sabbatical. We were once again entrepreneurs.

It only seemed natural to make this transition from ice cream to frozen yogurt. Frozen yogurt was the new "in" thing. The stores were the "hip" place to be with their cheery atmosphere, and even though customers piled on a vast variety of calorie-laden toppings, the perception was that frozen yogurt was healthy and low in calories and fat. The yogurt itself may have been low in calories and fat, but it was a rare customer who did not smother the yogurt with gummy bears and bits of Reese's Peanut Butter Cups, Snickers bars, and Butterfinger bars, ending up with a decadent dessert without the guilt—similar to the *Seinfeld* TV episode in which everyone was gaining weight because they were eating "nonfat" yogurt.

The store in Ogden did well the first year, and the reaction from customers was overwhelming. The store was lined with people eager to try this new dessert that offered the taste of ice cream without the calories or the guilt. With the early success in Ogden, we decided to expand as quickly as possible, and we opened three stores in Colorado (Denver, Colorado Springs, and Pueblo). My brother and another partner ran the stores in Colorado while my other brother, who lived in Boise, Idaho, did all the accounting.

The first couple years, the stores did well, as frozen yogurt was rapidly becoming more popular than ice cream. Unfortunately, we didn't have the foresight to see at the time that it was somewhat of a fad, and as with most fads, the novelty slowly diminished. And as the novelty of frozen yogurt waned, so did our sales.

Frozen-yogurt shops were suddenly appearing on every corner. The market was getting saturated, and frozen yogurt was no longer a novelty. Sales continued to decline—not a good thing in business! I loved owning and operating the shops and interacting with the customers, but we were making no money, paying ourselves just $1,000 per month, working long hours, and still losing money. I had gone from making $25,000 a year at McDonnell Douglas to $12,000 a year, and barely able to pay myself that amount. Those are the risks that come with owning your own business and being an entrepreneur. There are no guarantees. But I still loved it.

We could see the writing on the wall as sales continued to spiral downward. Unfortunately, the stores were expensive to get into, and because we had expanded too quickly, we still owed the bank money. We knew we had to get out of the frozen-yogurt business and sell the shops. Easier said than done.

To make matters worse, I had heard about a high-school classmate of mine who owned a multimillion dollar company, had a beautiful home, had a vacation home—and here I was in a business that was slowly going *out* of business. Not only did I have no money, I *owed* money to the banks. The only dream home I had was the one that was still tucked away in my suitcase. Rock bottom was getting closer by the day!

As I have gained some wisdom over the years, not only from the school of hard knocks but more importantly from the books I've read and the wisdom from all the teachers and masters mentioned in this book and countless others, I now know that the ego is something that can cause many of our problems and also can be the root cause of our suffering. Dissolving the ego is a fundamental teaching of most spiritual teachers, saints, and sages.

Perhaps fortunately for me at that time in my life, I didn't know much about the ego and its problems. I had not read any of these teachings. Consequently, my ego was still solidly intact and also kicked into massive overdrive after I heard about my high-school friend, saying things like, "How can this guy you knew in high school own a multimillion dollar business with a vacation home? How can he do it, and here you are with your little yogurt shop, making $12,000 a year? What are you doing? What have you done with your life? What happened to your dreams of becoming rich? Of becoming *anything*?" Business is all about growth, getting better, creativity, expanding, and ultimately about freedom, wealth, and success. We were experiencing the opposite.

MORE PLANTING

In a way which we do not understand, thoughts become things
just as seeds become plants. It is the mystery and miracle of
Life. Thoughts and mental attitudes become things.[55]
—Ernest Holmes

The day I heard the news about my high-school classmate being a millionaire was the day I told myself I was going to come up with something, some new business idea. I didn't care what it was, and I would work twenty hours a day if I had to. I was in my mid-thirties; I had no money, a business that was sinking like the Titanic, and a deep certainty that something had to change. I didn't have the faintest idea what this new venture might be, but I planted the seed that day that something greater was going to happen. It had to. I had drifted long enough.

Although I had no real job, no money saved, no career, and a child on the way, for some reason, I was never worried. I always felt there were plenty of ways to make money, and even though I didn't have any at the moment, it wasn't much of a concern. I had always lived well and liked the finer things in life, and I never felt like I was poor even when I was.

Back at Arizona State, I always had cash from my caddying. I always knew I could go out and make more money by getting more "loops" (a term for caddying eighteen holes). If I needed extra money, I would caddy thirty-six holes in one day instead of eighteen. None of my college friends had money to spend, but I always had cash.

Now, more than a decade later, I had that same mentality— that I could go out and make money. It might not be a career, but I knew I could get some type of job that would keep cash coming in. Despite my present condition of *being* poor, I never *felt* poor. Since I did like the finer things in life, I was always motivated to try to make more money. I'm not talking about owning a Ferrari and living in a mansion; for me, at that age, a nice apartment, a decent car, dinners at nice restaurants, a vacation now and then… that seemed like wealth.

I think society creates this illusion that if we haven't reached some level of success by our early to mid-thirties, maybe it just wasn't meant to be. Perhaps that is why we give up on our dreams too soon. Obviously, we all want and need money, a career, success (whatever that is to you), but just because you haven't reached it by a certain age doesn't mean you have to give up on your dreams. Even with my second business headed downhill, I still felt like I could make money—I just didn't know how or what it might be.

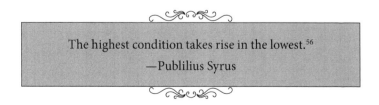

The highest condition takes rise in the lowest.[56]
—Publilius Syrus

THE BIG IDEA

Allowing creativity to unfold is very different from attempting
to force creativity through some kind of "technique.".…
For the light to enter, the mind must wander.[57]
—Scott Jeffrey

After my planting of the "any kind of new business" seed, several months passed. The yogurt shops continued to wane. One morning I was out running on the Mount Ogden trail above the Mount Ogden Golf Course. Running the trail was not only my way of exercising, but also a chance to be by myself, a way to let go of thinking and doing, to clear my mind. The trail was heavily wooded and was a great escape into nature, and also an escape from the trials and tribulations of life. I loved running on the Mount Ogden trail. It was my refuge, my freedom. But on this particular day, an idea appeared out of nowhere—an idea that made me stop running and jump around like a child at recess, a simple idea that got me so excited, I don't remember running home, and I don't remember being tired. Time as I knew it stood still.

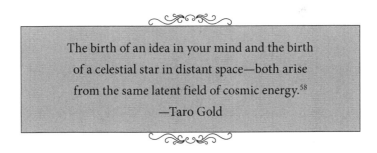

The birth of an idea in your mind and the birth
of a celestial star in distant space—both arise
from the same latent field of cosmic energy.[58]
—Taro Gold

So what was this wonderful idea? This epiphany? This grand vision? To chop Reese's Peanut Butter Cups into small pieces, put them in a box, and sell them! That was it. As simple as simple can be. You are probably saying, "Are you kidding? That got you so excited that you don't remember running home? Are you joking?"

And I will tell you why. In the yogurt shops, our best-selling topping for the frozen yogurt was the Reese's Peanut Butter Cups. Who doesn't like Reese's Peanut Butter Cups? Our customers obviously did. Yet we couldn't buy them already chopped. We had to go to a Costco or Sam's store, buy boxes of wrapped peanut-butter cups, unwrap them individually, and then chop them. The Reese's bin always seemed to be empty, and it was a major chore to unwrap and chop the cups to keep the bin full and our customers happy.

That day on the Mount Ogden running trail, the idea of someone chopping peanut-butter cups and putting them in a box for sale, to me, seemed like the greatest idea since sliced bread. I knew how hard it was to chop the cups on a daily basis. It was a never-ending battle. I knew there was a need for Reese's Peanut Butter Cups chopped in a convenient box. I knew the rest of the ice-cream and yogurt world had to be going through the same problems we had. I knew there was a need, and I was going to fill that need. I was going to work twenty hours a day if I had to. I was going to be the candy man.

After arriving back home from my run, I had to share my inspiration with someone. I was so excited. I immediately told my wife about it, and she liked the idea. But I was always bouncing ideas off her. Talking about an idea and actually taking action were two vastly different things. She had heard lots of my ideas—the key word being *heard*. But how often had I had taken action? That was another story.

I called my brother in Boise who was handling the accounting and bookkeeping for the yogurt shops. Let's just say he wasn't nearly as enthusiastic about the idea as I was. But he also didn't physically work in the stores to understand how hard it was to chop and keep the Reese's topping bins full. It did deflate my enthusiasm slightly, but I knew there was a need for this product. I knew I would buy it for our stores if it was available and that if I would buy it, so would other stores. So I called my brother in Colorado who was running two of our shops, and he loved the idea. We talked at length about the possibilities, and about all the potential customers for chopped peanut-butter cups. My excitement was back, and back for good.

The seed that I had planted on that close-to-rock-bottom day where it seemed as if my life was falling apart was now starting to see the light of day. The seed was now becoming more than a seed. Chopped Reese's Peanut Butter Cups were thinking about emerging from the soil. But as with all ideas, this was still just an idea until I took action. I could either continue to drift and do nothing, or I could take action. I chose to take action.

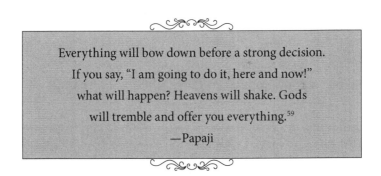

Everything will bow down before a strong decision.
If you say, "I am going to do it, here and now!"
what will happen? Heavens will shake. Gods
will tremble and offer you everything.[59]
—Papaji

I was ready to take action, but there was something in the back of my mind that also seemed to be trying to hold me back. *You can't really do this. Are there laws about putting product in boxes? Label laws? Interstate laws? How are you going to ship it? Are there health laws?* All kinds of doubt about why I shouldn't or couldn't do it rolled in. But even though I had not yet heard of Vernon Howard, I wound up taking his advice, which is, "The best way to start doing something is to start doing something."[60]

I just started chopping. I bought a knife, a cutting board, a bucket, labels, boxes, bags and some Reese's Peanut Butter Cups and started chopping. I do want to point out that I was fortunate that when I started the business, the regulations and quality programs didn't compare to today's standards. We now have eight people in our quality-assurance department; when I started, I only vaguely knew what quality assurance even was. So I don't recommend jumping in quite as quickly as I did, but you can still do as Vernon Howard says and start doing "something" to get your business off the ground, or whatever endeavor you are interested in. You can take precautions and do your due diligence, but start doing something.

I rented a small space in an old cold-storage warehouse in Ogden. The first day, it was ninety-plus degrees outside. The warehouse had no air conditioning, and my wife and I spent a whole day chopping ten-pound cases of peanut-butter cups. We were hot, tired, and a bit disillusioned. I didn't think it would be that hard. A whole day of work, and we only got through thirty-seven cases.

That night, I called my brother in Colorado and told him that it was too much work, too hard. I didn't think I could do it. His reply, which is vividly etched in my mind, was, "You have to!" Easy for him to say, five hundred miles away. But he knew it was our only way out. He knew there was a market for the product. He knew it would be our new dream fulfilled. And deep down, so did I. And I needed that kick in the…

The next day was better. My wife and I were getting better and faster. I was excited again. Our first customer was a company in Southern California. They were the supplier of the yogurt and toppings for our yogurt shops, and the largest distributor in Southern California for yogurt and ice-cream stores. I had talked to the buyer about my idea, and she was willing to give it a shot. One of the best phone calls I have ever received was when the buyer called me after the first two weeks of selling the chopped peanut-butter cups and saying our product was "flying" out the doors, and that we had "the hottest thing going." I was ecstatic.

All my thoughts and dreams were focused on this new business. I was living and breathing chopped Reese's. It's all I could think about. I was going to do whatever it took. If I had to work twenty hours a day, I was going to do it. This was the seed I had planted. It was slowly starting to bloom. And to me, it was the most beautiful sight in the world.

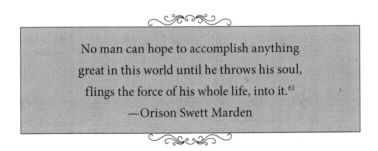

No man can hope to accomplish anything great in this world until he throws his soul, flings the force of his whole life, into it.[61]
—Orison Swett Marden

Despite pouring my heart and soul into the business, there wasn't enough income yet for me to work full-time at it. We were in the process of selling our frozen yogurt shops, and I had enrolled at the University of Utah to get a master's degree in engineering (just in case this little chopping business didn't work out). I was also getting a monthly stipend from the university—I'm still not sure how or why—paying me to go to college. I also had my first child on the way. You can imagine how my mother-in-law must have felt when she would come to visit and see her pregnant daughter and "engineer" son-in-law chopping peanut-butter cups with butcher knives in the back of an old warehouse! What happened to the aeronautical engineer her daughter had been engaged to? Where did that guy go? She was a great sport, however, and always encouraged me.

I want to mention that my brother in Boise who was skeptical at first turned out to be invaluable in getting the business started and arranging financing from the bank. Most accountants are hesitant and skeptical by nature—with good reason—and he was just being a good accountant. If the business was to grow, financing from the bank was critical. The business would not be where it is today without the help of both my brothers, who are equal partners in the business. We all have strengths that have complimented each other's in a good way.

As the business grew, I hired a couple of college students to help me chop. I, along with another employee, could now chop a hundred of the ten-pound cases of peanut-butter cups in a day. One thousand pounds a day. It wasn't easy, but again, it never felt like work. I would get home at night and couldn't wait to get back the next day. To this day, I never say I am going to "work," because it has never felt like work. It has always felt like building a dream, creating my freedom—never like just a job.

Never work.[62]
—Guy Debord

Fortunately, we were able to sell three of the four yogurt shops and closed the fourth. We were out of the frozen-yogurt business and now we were in the toppings business. It was another step in what seemed like a natural transition from ice cream to frozen yogurt to toppings. The great thing about this new business venture was that it took very little money to get started. If it didn't work out, the financial impact was minimal. The main cash outlay was for the inventory (Reese's Peanut Butter Cups), and once they were chopped and sold, the money came back from the customer. It didn't require a big investment for a building, new equipment, a franchise fee—just a bucket, a knife, cutting board, boxes, and peanut-butter cups. After our venture in the yogurt business and still owing money to the bank, it was the only way we could get back in business unless we had outside investors.

One of the most important lessons we learned from our experience in the frozen-yogurt business was to be very careful about borrowing money and to not get in over our heads by expanding too quickly. Many businesses take a significant amount of money to get started before you even know how the business will do. With the yogurt franchise, we had an initial franchise fee—which can be substantial—and, depending on the franchise, you may have a major investment in the building or build-out of the store, as well as the equipment and everything else you need to get started.

You obviously need to do your research on the franchise you are getting into. One of the advantages of owning a franchise is that they have, in most cases, been in business for a while, with an established track record. Unfortunately, the frozen-yogurt business was relatively new, didn't have a long track record, and cost a lot of money to get into. At least, it was a lot of money to us.

If you are starting a new business, I would highly recommend starting small if you can and see how it does. Our big mistake was borrowing too much money to get started and rushing to open more stores. We got caught up in the initial excitement and sales and thought it would last forever. I guess it was just part of the school of hard knocks, but it was a costly education. When you start your own business, if at all possible use your own money to get started. I do recommend establishing a relationship (line of credit) with a bank to fund growth, inventory, etc. You don't want to go out of business the first year because you didn't have adequate financing, but be careful how quickly you expand and how much you borrow.

When I was starting this new business venture, I was chopping peanut-butter cups, going to school, and also taking odd jobs to help bring in some extra cash flow. I was not putting all my eggs in one basket, even though I believed passionately in what I was doing. I worked hard at the various "labor" jobs I had while getting the business started, but all my thoughts and soul were in the new business, TR Toppers. As a side note, it was my wife who came up with the name for the business, which did have a ring to it—primarily because it had my initials at the beginning. Again, the ego at work! As I mentioned, I had not yet learned or heard of the teachings in this book, so my ego wasn't dissolved. It was still active and thriving.

My brothers and I were continually trying to sell the chopped peanut-butter cups to any customers we could think of who might buy our product. After two years of chopping by hand, I called a major national ice-cream company, told them about our chopped peanut-butter cups, and quoted them a price—and they gave us a contract for their spring promotion! All over the phone. They hadn't seen the product, had never met or talked to me, had not inspected our warehouse, knew nothing about us, and yet they approved our pricing and gave us a purchase order. Keep in mind, this was over twenty years ago. It would never happen today; there are countless rules and regulations, audits… no, this was a once-in-a-lifetime chance.

Their order was for 140,000 pounds of chopped peanut-butter cups, and they would need it in two months! I almost dropped the phone. I was in shock. Of course I told them we could do it, even though at the time we were chopping a thousand pounds a day by hand in the back of an old warehouse, and I knew what I was agreeing to was virtually impossible. As Julia Cameron writes in *The Artist's Way,* "Anyone honest will tell you that possibility is far more interesting than impossibility."[63]

I had blocked out the impossibility and saw nothing but possibility. I had blinders on. Quickly doing the math in my head (finally using my engineering), I quickly figured out that this would take 140 days straight without any other business. How could I possibly have told them we could do it? We had to do something different, and we had to do it fast. It was time to get a dicing machine. It was time to get serious about becoming the candy man.

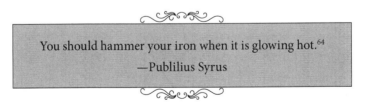

You should hammer your iron when it is glowing hot.[64]
—Publilius Syrus

The only problem I had with the dicing machine (besides the fact that it was expensive, which is why we hadn't purchased one before) was that when I was chopping by hand, my chop was perfect. There were no fines, the pieces were well defined, and it looked great. I was concerned that a dicing machine could not possibly chop the product as perfectly as I did.

We sent samples to the company that made the dicing machine, and they sent their chopped samples back. Their samples looked good, but not as good as my "perfect" hand chop! I was afraid our customers would not like the product as well and that we would lose sales. But we had to do something different. We had this huge order and only a month to get it done. We had to get automated. And the only ways to do it were to purchase a dicing machine or have a warehouse full of employees with knives and buckets. We opted for the dicing machine. And as it turned out, it was a wise decision.

The new machine revolutionized the business. Once we got the machine, my brother from Colorado came to help with our 140,000 pound order that now needed to be finished in three weeks. Two of the employees who had worked with me when I chopped by hand also helped. The four of us chopped peanut-butter cups for twenty-one straight days, working twelve-hour days. The new machine was great, but it was still physically demanding to open 140,000 pounds of peanut-butter cups and run them through a dicing machine, and then package and palletize the product.

Physically it was the hardest thing I have ever done over that length of time, but again, it never felt like work. Sure the days were long, it was hot and physically demanding—but if what you are doing is what you truly want to do, and you pour your heart and soul into it, you will never think of it as work. This applies to whatever you do. In writing this book, at times it was hard to initially to sit down to write, but once I start writing, there was no work. Time seems to be nonexistent. You forget about time—unless you have to chop 140,000 pounds of peanut-butter cups and have a deadline!

You certainly don't have to be an entrepreneur to experience this feeling. You could have what you feel is the greatest job in the world and love what you do, and you also would never call it work. If you feel this way, you've probably chosen the perfect career for you.

We accomplished what we had to do, and what an accomplishment it was. We chopped 140,000 pounds of peanut-butter cups, we fulfilled our commitment to this major ice-cream company, we got them their product when they needed it, and we survived twenty-one straight days of chopping. I have never felt that kind of satisfaction. It was a euphoric feeling of accomplishment, pride, relief, joy, and happiness. That was over twenty years ago, and despite many great things happening with the business and my love for it, I haven't had that same sense of overwhelming pride and accomplishment. How did we pull it off? We had to.

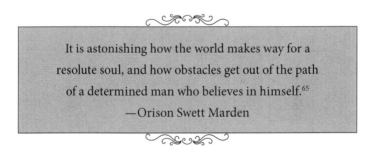

It is astonishing how the world makes way for a resolute soul, and how obstacles get out of the path of a determined man who believes in himself.[65]
—Orison Swett Marden

It's true, the dicing machine didn't chop the peanut-butter cups as perfectly as my hand chop, but no customers complained, and it was the turning point for the business and our ability to grow and expand. We decided to relocate to Pueblo, Colorado, where my brother Greg was living. Pueblo was centrally located in the country for shipping our product to both the East and

West coasts and also to the Midwest. Another big break came when we started supplying Dairy Queen nationally for their Blizzard program. We also started chopping more toppings, such as M&Ms, Snickers bars, Butterfinger bars, Heath bars… business was booming.

We did everything: chopping, sales, building orders, loading trucks, entering orders, customer service—and despite long days, it still never seemed like work. I would get home at night and was living and breathing chopped candy. The seed that I planted back in Ogden when it appeared we were close to rock bottom was now growing and getting bigger every day, every month, every year. We were and are the candy men, and it all came from a seed that later emerged as an idea, and when the idea was acted on, it became a reality. From the invisible to the visible. I had gone from drifting to taking action. I was using universal powers, but I still didn't know it.

Our business has grown from an idea, a knife, a cutting board, and some Reese's Peanut Butter Cups into a company that now sells over 100 million dollars annually and has over three hundred toppings that are distributed throughout the United States and internationally. Our customers include Dairy Queen, Sonic, Dreyer's/Edy's, McDonald's, Baskin-Robbins, bakeries, restaurants, frozen-yogurt and ice-cream chains, as well as hundreds of distributors. I tell you this not to boast but to show that I started with nothing but a knife and an idea. I could have let the idea come and go like lots of others that I had, but I knew it was time to take action. I also want to show that you don't have to have money, you don't have to "know someone," you don't have to have wealthy parents, you don't have to have been born into the right family. Anyone can do it.

You might wonder why the candy business has grown and thrived while the other ventures we were in were relatively short-lived. I don't necessarily have an answer, but maybe it's because we didn't have the business experience, the business savvy, the wisdom, the "hard knocks" when we took on those earlier enterprises. Or perhaps it's nature's way of not giving us too much at an early age. The intelligence of the universe protected us from ourselves until we had time to mature, gain wisdom, and possibly learn about some of the ideas in this book.

Personally, I believe it would have been a disaster if I had made a lot of money when I was younger. If you achieve wealth and fame at an early age, what do you do next? We all have read stories about rock stars, athletes, actors, and actresses who became famous when they were young, with money pouring in from all directions, and wound up in rehab centers for drug abuse and alcohol abuse, many eventually losing all their money. Early business struggles could be nature's way of trying to protect us until we are wise enough to be able to handle good fortune or wealth—so we don't wind up in rehab.

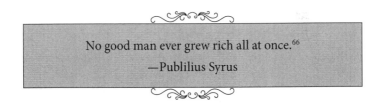

No good man ever grew rich all at once.[66]
—Publilius Syrus

But I think I have a better idea why the candy business has been successful for all these years. The other businesses were businesses that were started by someone else. We didn't come up with the concept of ice-cream trucks or frozen yogurt. They were just channels for us to get into business—to become entrepreneurs again—but nothing that *we* created, nothing that we poured our heart and soul into to make it a reality.

I equate the candy business to your children. The idea was the conception, and we raised and nurtured the business from the beginning, learning every nuance that was associated with it. It wasn't established. We had to raise this business just as you would raise a child. We had to slowly bring it along, learning as we went, experiencing the highs and lows. There is not a business in the world that we could have loved more, just as with your children. This was our baby. Our project. Our dream. Our freedom. That's why it has endured all these years. That's why we're still chopping candy twenty years later. It's part of the family.

I hope the experiences I've shared in this section will in some way help you in your life, in *your* story. My intention with this part of the book was to not only give you a background on things that have transpired in my life but also show you how I have drifted, how I have taken action, and how I have on a few occasions, unknowingly, used some of the powers that are the central theme of this book. These are extremely simple powers and laws that so few of us know anything about or are aware of. We go through our entire lives living from our five senses, never going beyond to the place where untold possibilities exist—where all of creation is.

Just think what you might be able to do if you learned, studied, and practiced some of these teachings that are in this book and countless others. What if you became aware of why things happen the way they do in your life, became able to create your life with this knowledge, became the captain of your ship, and every day became a greater you. Just think of the possibilities and the freedom, limitless and without boundaries. That's our true nature. That's who we really are. And that's why I wrote this book—not to bore you with past accomplishments in my life, with a story that is not a story at all, with my tales of being the ice-cream man, the yogurt man, or the candy man.

Mastery over life is not attained by dominion over material things, but by mental perception of their true cause and nature. The wise man does not attempt to bend the world to fit his way but strives for a higher consciousness that enables him to perceive the secret cause behind all things.[67]
—U. S. Andersen

The good, the bad, and the ugly—I created it all, and so do you. I just didn't know how or why at that time, but I do now. I hope the rest of this book enlightens you and allows you to rise above the bad and the ugly and focus on the good and the greater. Because you are the captain. You create your reality.

And as a side note, speaking of seeds that were planted and using universal powers, I *do* live in that house that I cut out of the paper on that sunny poolside day in Las Vegas. It's no longer a thought, a dream, a wadded-up piece of paper stuffed in my suitcase. I located the builder of the home, bought the plans, and built that exact house, in which I live now. All from planting a seed. I had no idea that I was planting the house seed, but as I said in the beginning, I did occasionally use these universal laws unknowingly, and if you plant and nourish the right seeds, it's amazing the possibilities that can blossom. But you can't make a seed grow any faster than nature allows. In this case, the house seed took many years, but it did bloom. And I am living in the seed that I planted.

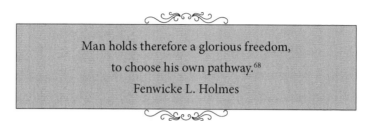

Man holds therefore a glorious freedom,
to choose his own pathway.[68]
Fenwicke L. Holmes

4

Business

I am like any other man. All I do is supply a demand.[69]

—Al Capone

There are a number of reasons that I have included "Business" as a chapter in this book—the number-one reason being that the majority of my life has centered around being an entrepreneur. The purpose of this chapter is to share some specific insight that I have acquired in business over my lifetime that I feel includes some of the key fundamentals of our business successes and business in general. I also want to show that business is not complicated. This is not a business book, but what I want to show is that not only is business simple, there are also some simple, inexpensive things you can do to make your business or service great that are often glossed over and not given enough attention.

> I've heard it said that an entrepreneur is someone
> who will work 24 hours a day for themselves to
> avoid working one hour for someone else.[70]
> —Chris Guillebeau

Regardless of our occupation or situation in life, we're all involved in business transactions. Whether you are selling yourself (for a job), art, books, crafts, your church, your knowledge, your services—all throughout our lives, we all are involved in sales in some fashion. We are also all consumers. We buy from these same people that I am talking about who are selling their wares. We buy and sell things—that's the crux of business. It isn't complicated. There are many books that seem to want to make business more complicated than it is or needs to be, but the bottom line is: business is simple. And the more simple you make it, the more successful you will be, and the happier you will be too. If you want to screw up your business, make it complicated. It will not only make your business much more difficult to run, but your personal life will suffer as well.

So what is the crux of business? *Offering something to someone else who needs that something and is willing to pay you for it.* That's it. That's business. Simplicity at its best. Obviously there are many other factors to making a business successful, but if you can fill a need and people will pay you for it, you're in business! The mobster "Lucky" Luciano is quoted as saying, "If you have a lot of what people want and can't get, then you can supply the demand and shovel in the dough."[71] Though I'm not condoning the kind of business Lucky was in, I do like that quote. That's exactly what business is: offering what people want and can't get, with great service.

Universities, books, authors, professors, business people—all have tried their best to make business much more complicated, and it scares people away. They love making it complicated. I have read many business books, or attempted to; after the first few chapters or even the first few pages, I couldn't read anymore. Why? They were too complicated, too long, too hard, too much, too boring. One example is *In Search of Excellence.*[72] It's been said it's one of the greatest business books of all time, but for me, It was too long, too complicated, and too boring. Maybe I should have tried to read more of the book, but after the first chapter, I couldn't go any further. I realize that's not a fair critique of a book, but for me, it was too much. I didn't want business to be that complicated.

I have heard renowned author and speaker Larry Winget say, "If you can't explain what you do for a living in one sentence, then you don't know what you do for a living." What do I do? I chop and sell candy. Larry would be proud of my brief summary! I rarely read business books now, but Larry Winget is one author I would recommend. He's like the Mafia guys—in a good way—in that he is direct, in your face, keeps things simple, and offers sound advice. He is no-nonsense. No fluff. Just the basics. If you own a business, are thinking of starting one, or are going to college to study business, check out Larry's books. Even if you aren't going into business, you will be wiser after reading them.

In business, I have always believed that if you have just a *marginal* product or service, decent location and advertising, and exceptional customer service, your business will be successful. If you have a *great* product or service, decent location, and exceptional customer service, your business will boom. To give you an example, let's say you have a hot-dog vending business on a busy street corner in a major city. As long as your hot dogs are good and you offer great customer service, your business should do well. Now let's say you have the best hot dogs in the city and also offer fresh lobster sandwiches as well, and you give all your customers exceptional customer service—that is, you get to know their names, treat them like royalty on every visit, make a point of showing them how much you appreciate their business—and your customers will be lined up around the block.

There obviously are other aspects of business that are important, which I will discuss, but exceptional/extraordinary customer service will take you farther in business than anything else, as long as you have a product or service that people want. I have been in business as an entrepreneur for twenty-five years (and if you include night crawlers, caddying, and my other odd jobs, most of my life has centered around being an entrepreneur) and the bottom line is, if you can fill a need for someone else and offer them exceptional customer service, then you are on your way to becoming a successful entrepreneur or businessperson.

I will briefly discuss what I believe are the most important aspects of business. I don't want to overcomplicate it. I will give you key fundamentals that have been critical to our business success. I am also in no way implying that you don't need to go to college or read business books. Maybe *In Search of Excellence* will help you. Everything you learn about business will help. When I was first starting out in business, I read every business book I could get my hands on. But you don't have to go to college or read hundreds of business books to be successful in business. Bill Gates and Steve Jobs both dropped out of college and started businesses, and they seemed to do okay!

I personally don't remember too much about my college courses in business (my minor), but I do remember what *wasn't* said. There was virtually nothing said about customer service. Not one course on customer service. The most important aspect of any business—along with a good product or service—and there's barely a mention of it in college business courses.

How can colleges overlook something so critical and vital to business success? If I owned a college and had a business school, it would be a requirement to have at least two semesters on customer service. Customer Service 101 and 102. Even if you spent the entire semester on different ways to say thank you. Nothing complicated—just the basics. Go through any fast-food drive-thru in the country, with the exception of chains like Starbucks, In-N-Out Burger, and a few others, and you will see why these courses would be mandatory.

I would make all business students (in my imaginary university) in the master's program do a portion of their final thesis on customer service. It wouldn't matter if you were studying accounting, economics, or any other field in business—you would be required to take courses in customer service. Everyone in a company should be part of and embrace the extraordinary customer service of the company. No one should be excluded.

Choose to deliver amazing service to your customers. You'll stand out because they don't get it anywhere else.[73]
—Kevin Stirtz

I can't emphasize enough the importance of customer service. It doesn't matter what business or service you provide—exceptional customer service should be one of your top priorities. It's your cheapest form of advertising. It's the least expensive improvement you can make in your business, and yet most businesses seem oblivious to their poor customer service.

There is no easier way to lose a customer forever than by having poor customer service. Again, there has to be a demand for your goods or services, but that should be obvious. Great customer service is not so obvious, and that is why it is lacking in most businesses. Why is it so often overlooked? Maybe because it isn't taught in school. It's not something we learn in our educational system, not in college, and not in high school either. All students graduating from high school and college will at some point in their lives be involved in business—whether as an employer, employee, consumer—and yet we are not taught one of the most fundamental aspects of any business.

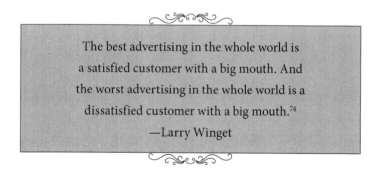

The best advertising in the whole world is a satisfied customer with a big mouth. And the worst advertising in the whole world is a dissatisfied customer with a big mouth.[74]
—Larry Winget

If you own your own business, it's your responsibility as an owner to ensure your employees are trained with exceptional customer-service skills—and more importantly, your management. It's your responsibility to create a culture centered around great customer service. It costs virtually nothing to implement, and you can drastically change your business and ultimately your bottom line. Never put off extraordinary customer service for some time in the future. Do it today.

> Although your customers won't love you if you
> give bad service, your competitor will.[75]
> —Kate Zebriskie

Basic customer service rules that we try to instill in our company are:

- Treat the customer like a king or queen.
- Treat each customer like he or she is the most important customer you have.
- Make customers feel special.
- Return customers' phone calls promptly and respond to their e-mails promptly.
- Act excited when you talk to customers (you should be excited, because they are paying you).
- Follow through on all customer requests in a timely manner.
- Never overpromise, and always do what you say you are going to do.
- Put your best customer-service employees in positions in which they are dealing with customers directly.
- Customers' requests should be top priority for everyone in the company.
- Always say thank you. It's amazing to me how often employees of companies fail to do this.

If you only incorporate two things into a new customer-service program, my recommendation would be to treat the customer like a king or queen—like the most important customer you have—and say thank you. Those two simple things will do wonders for your business.

DON'T GO INTO BUSINESS JUST FOR THE MONEY

You know you are on the road to success if you would do your job, and not be paid for it.[76]
—Oprah Winfrey

First, let me say that anyone who goes into business wants to make money. If the business doesn't make money, you won't be in business long. So making money is critical to all good businesses. But if you are looking into becoming an entrepreneur and your *sole* motivation for starting a business is for the money, you need to do something else, because the odds are good that it won't work out. Sure, everyone wants to make money, and everyone thinks that owning a business is the ticket to wealth and happiness. It definitely can be—if you don't do it "just for the money."

Most people starting a new business think about opening a restaurant because they can't come up with any other business ideas. You may know nothing about the restaurant business, but I think people who haven't been in business are under the illusion that restaurants make a lot of money. We had the same illusion when we got into the frozen-yogurt business. It appeared, since there were so many customers in the stores, that the frozen-yogurt shops had to be making a killing. What most people don't understand—including us, before we got in over our heads—is that the restaurant business is extremely competitive, requires long hours, is expensive to get into, and doesn't bring in as much money as you might think (unless you own several or one "great" one). Most are open at least 360 days a year. Bottom line is, they require a ton of work.

Now, if you are an aspiring chef, love food and cooking, love and know the restaurant industry—then you are much more likely to be successful. The same is true for any business you get into. But you don't have to have a passion for the business that you are getting into. I didn't have a "passion" for chopping Reese's Peanut Butter Cups. Who could have a passion for chopping peanut-butter cups? But I did have a passion for being an entrepreneur, a passion for freedom, a passion for making deals, and a passion for making my ideas a reality.

When first starting the business I own now with my two brothers, I had grandiose dreams and visions for its success, but I was never obsessed by the money. Anyone who goes into business wants to make money, and I would be lying if I said that wasn't a motivating factor for me (since I always wanted to be rich). But my point is, you don't want to focus exclusively on the money. I knew the money would come if I could make the business the best it could be every day. I never worried about the outcome—well, occasionally, but not often. I was too excited about the business.

I worked for an oil and gas company in the mid-eighties, and the owner used to tell me that during the oil boom, his feet hit the floor running when he got out of bed every morning. That's how excited he was to go to his business each day. That's the way I felt and still do.

> Happiness lies not in the mere possession
> of money; it lies in the joy of achievement,
> in the thrill of the creative effort.[77]
> —Franklin D. Roosevelt

That's passion. That's what will make you successful. That's what they don't and can't teach you in business school. It's something you feel, not something you learn. It's when you just worked twelve to fifteen hours in your business and you get home and you can't wait to get back the next day. It's all you think and talk about. You have your heart and soul in it. That's what will make you a successful entrepreneur. That's what will cause the money to flow in. You don't have to have a passion for the specific business you're in, but if you have a passion for business, for being an entrepreneur, for the excitement, for building dreams, for the risk and reward, for being creative… then you might think about starting a business. But don't do it "just for the money." Don't do anything "just for the money," because in the end, the money won't be there.

> You know, my main reaction to this money thing is that
> it's humorous, all the attention to it, because it's hardly the
> most insightful or valuable thing that's happened to me.[78]
> —Steve Jobs

> Money was never a big motivation for me, except as a way to keep score. The real excitement is playing the game.[79]
> —Donald Trump

A GOOD MONEY PERSON

If you are not an accountant, if you don't like dealing with the small details, and yet you want to start your own business, hire the best "money person" you can afford. If you can't afford it, you may need to go to the library or go to the Internet and read everything you can on managing your finances in your business. I would recommend finding someone to help, even part-time, if you are not good with the details and accounting. It's critical to your success in business. You can have the greatest product or service in the world, but if you don't manage the finances with care, your business will not only suffer but probably won't survive. You need to know where every dollar is going. If you can't do it yourself, hire someone that can.

My advice, without going into great detail, is to get counseling from an accountant and have that individual set you up with the financial and accounting tools that are necessary for your business. It's not an area of expertise for me, and I was fortunate to have a brother who was an accountant and has taken care of all the minute details that are necessary to run a successful business. He does it very well. I recognize the importance of it, and that is why I am conveying this message to you.

FAILURE

There is no such thing as failure, only feedback.[80]
—Michael Gelb

I know you think I am going to say that in order to succeed, you must first experience failure. It's business-book basics to say that you need to fail to succeed. Who hasn't heard that? But I am here to tell you that I have never failed, unless I didn't try. If I didn't try, if I didn't give it my best, and things didn't work out, then I failed. As long as I gave something my full attention and effort, there was no failure. I always learned something from every experience—even if the only thing I learned was, "It's time to close the doors because it's not working!"

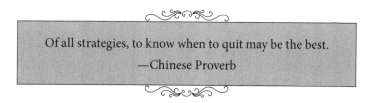

Of all strategies, to know when to quit may be the best.
—Chinese Proverb

Our adventure in the frozen-yogurt business might appear to have been a failure. At the time, it felt like failure. It felt like a disaster. It felt like rock bottom. But we worked hard, gave it our best shot, and it just didn't work out. We didn't fail. Frozen yogurt was on the way out in the early nineties, and so were we. Even though we lost money, we learned valuable business lessons. And the best thing? It catapulted us into our current business. Sometimes you have to find hidden gems in what appears to be a hopeless situation (see chapter 11, "The Beauty of Rock Bottom"). In this case, what appeared to be a failure led to something far greater.

> I have not failed. I've just found 10,000
> ways that won't work.[81]
> —Thomas Edison

Never consider any business venture or anything you do in life a failure as long as you have given it your best effort, your best shot. If you don't, *then* you can call it a failure. Obviously these are my thoughts on failure and my personal definition. If you want to consider what you have done as a failure, I certainly can't stop you. But if you tried and gave it your best, I would be hesitant about labeling it a failure.

KEY EMPLOYEES

You're not the only pebble on the beach.[82]
—Harry Braisted

There will always be employees in any business who believe the business couldn't survive without them. They believe that if they were to leave, the business would fall apart the day they walked out the door. They are also a bit delusional.

In the 1997 movie *Donnie Brasco*, the character of Lefty Ruggiero, played by Al Pacino, says, "I'm a spoke on a wheel. And so was he, and so are you."[83] You could say that about just about anybody in a business. When a spoke falls off a wheel, what do you do? You replace it. It may take a while to find the perfect replacement—the best spoke you can get. No one in business likes to lose key people. At the time, it may seem devastating. And you may even have thoughts that the business can't survive without this particular employee.

Throughout our business career, we have had key employees—I hate to say "key," because they are all key—who have left for another job or various reasons, and also employees who we had to fire (not because of their job performance, but for other extenuating circumstances). And there was always a feeling of, *What are we going to do now? Was this employee critical to our success? Can we survive without this person?* And the answer to all of these questions is that not only did the business survive, but most of the time we replaced the employee with someone who was actually better—more skilled, more talented—and brought a new perspective to the business. The business "wheel" kept on turning, a little more efficiently and smoothly. Our worries were for naught.

You will find a replacement. The wheel will keep on turning just as well with the new spoke as it did with the old one. The next time you either lose a key employee or think you *are* that key employee, think again. You're just another spoke on the wheel.

MULTITASKING

I've heard it said that multitasking means "screwing everything up simultaneously." I would advise against it. Multitasking implies that you are trying to do several things at once. It sounds nice. People like to use the word. It sounds important to do several things at once. However, as a consequence, usually nothing is done very well.

How many times have you been on the phone with someone in business (or anywhere now) and while they are talking to you they are checking e-mails, texts, surfing the Web—giving you, at best, 50 percent of their attention. It's annoying and rude. Not only are they "half there" for the conversation with you, but they are only "half there" for the e-mail or text they may be sending while talking to you. There's no benefit to doing two things at once in a half-ass manner, and it's not good business.

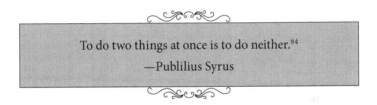

To do two things at once is to do neither.[84]
—Publilius Syrus

Stop the multitasking and become great at one thing instead of mediocre at two or three. Next time you interview prospective employees for your company, don't ask them if they can multitask—ask them what they are great at one thing at a time.

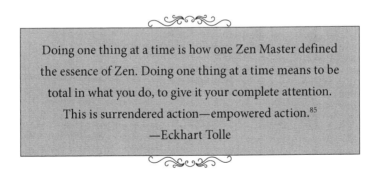

Doing one thing at a time is how one Zen Master defined the essence of Zen. Doing one thing at a time means to be total in what you do, to give it your complete attention. This is surrendered action—empowered action.[85]
—Eckhart Tolle

PASSION

If we focus on our highest goal, our
passion comes to us effortlessly.[86]
—Michael Ray

I write about passion because almost every business book or motivational speech given to high school and college graduates tells you to "follow your passion" in life. We have all heard this line. There is nothing wrong with this advice, as you do want to be inspired by whatever you may choose to do in your life. I too would encourage you to follow your passion—*if you know what your passion truly is*. But it can also be misleading.

One of my passions when I graduated from college was golf. But I knew I wasn't going to be a professional golfer. I didn't want to open or work in a golf shop. I liked "playing" golf. I know many avid golfers who have opened their own business selling golf equipment, working at a golf course in the pro shop, and they spent all their time working, leaving little time to actually play the game. I also knew of a few golf fanatics who had to close their golf shops.

This doesn't just apply to golf. My point is that just because your passion may be golf, tennis, dancing, music, it doesn't mean you *have* to work in that field. I personally knew that if I could build my own business, work for myself, create my own reality, that I would be able to actually "play" golf, or travel, or write, or do all the things that I love to do. That's how I could follow my passions. Don't go into the tennis business because you like playing tennis. Do it because that's all you ever wanted to do— to work, play, and always be involved in tennis. Apply this to whatever career path you choose.

> It is the soul's duty to be loyal to its own desires.
> It must abandon itself to its master passion.[87]
> —Rebecca West

Make sure you know what your passion really is before you just blindly pursue something because you believe it is your passion. As I said, chopping Reese's Peanut Butter Cups was never my passion, but it gave me the freedom in my life to pursue and play in all my other passions. I became passionate about my business, and chopping peanut-butter cups just happened to be the cornerstone of the business.

My son, who plays college tennis, loves the game but is even more passionate about music. If he could find a job in the music industry, he would be in heaven. But jobs in the music industry are scarce, and selling guitars in a music store eight hours a day is not where his passion lies. So I always ask him what he feels is missing in the music industry today. What is needed? What is the biggest problem with music today? All of these questions get him thinking about a niche that isn't being filled. It gets him thinking like an entrepreneur about something he is passionate about.

Maybe he will get a job working at a tennis club to keep some money coming in, but he can still focus on his highest goal of being involved in music someday and perhaps maybe even coming up with the next iTunes! By the way, when I asked him what he thought was one of the biggest problems with the music industry today, what was needed, he mentioned iTunes and its monopoly, lack of customer service, no one to talk to, and high prices. I'm not sure if he will be able to take on the behemoth Apple, but you never know. A tiny seed was planted.

When I started chopping Reese's, it ignited a passion in me. I knew chopping peanut-butter cups wasn't the perfect job or the perfect career path. I also knew it wasn't my passion in life. But it kindled a blaze within me, and the world did seem to rearrange itself to bring me what I was seeking, and much faster than I expected. It ignited a passion in me. If you want to study quotes about passion, I would put this one by Srikumar Rao in the middle of your desk or on your refrigerator door and read it every day:

> Here is an immutable truth for you to ponder: Passion does not exist in the job. It exists in you—and if you cannot ignite it within yourself right where you are now, you will never find it outside yourself. It is futile to search frantically for that perfect position. Paradoxically, when you discover the truth of this and begin to kindle the blaze within yourself, the external world rearranges itself to bring you what you seek and usually much faster than you expected.[88]

It sums up nicely what I have been trying to say: that the passion doesn't exist in the job, it is in you regardless, of the career path you take. It's up to you to ignite it.

THE MYTHICAL TOP

When you reach the top, keep climbing.[89]
—Chinese Proverb

In business and in life, there is no top rung. You will never reach the top. You can come close, but you will never reach it. It's like seeking enlightenment—you don't want to achieve it. You don't want to get to the very top. Because then what would you do? You can retire, but deep down you'd know that you never reached the pinnacle of what you were trying to achieve. Again, you can come close, but our inherent need is for self-expression and self-expansion. In business, there is not an ultimate dollar figure that you're trying to reach and then you can retire. Business, as in life, is all about getting better, creating new things, expanding, growing, not reaching some mythical top. You want to be better every day, every month, every year. That's your real goal—not a dollar figure.

In his book *The 50 Year Dash*, Bob Greene wrote this about the top rung:

> There is no top rung that makes you feel that the climb is finished. Wherever you think the finish line may be, you will be wrong. If the top rung really did feel like the top rung, it would be good and it would be bad. Good because it would finally settle you, let you exhale. Bad because it would do away with ambition.
>
> And even knowing the top rung is illusory, you keep pulling yourself toward it. Because there is no alternative to that pursuit, or at least none that you are aware of, so you continue on your climb, not knowing what lies ahead.
>
> The truth is that at 50, you become finally aware that there is no top rung to that ladder you've been on. If you're waiting to reach the top rung, you can forget it, because it doesn't exist.[90]

Not knowing what lies ahead is where the excitement is. When I first started TR Toppers, it was just as much fun and as exciting as it is today. Each year we tried to improve, think of new products, new ideas—anything we could do to grow the business. And we do the same thing today. It's never been about a final destination, a final resting place. It's always been about growth, getting better, creating, not just a final number and then we will be happy. It's all about the process. The journey. The adventure.

Reaching a goal provides satisfaction, but it won't last. The only thing that will last is your continuous climb up the ladder to ever greater heights. That's where the excitement and fun is. We all need and want the climb. You won't reach your top rung, but that doesn't mean you can't come close. Keep climbing.

5

Elegance

For me, elegance is not to pass unnoticed but to
get to the very soul of what one is.[91]
—Christian Lacroix

Elegance is a strange word and concept, because it is difficult to
define exactly what it is. How do you know if something is elegant?
Definitions from the Encarta Dictionary are:

(1) **Style and good taste** A combination of graceful stylishness,
distinction, and good taste in appearance, behavior, or
movement.
(2) **Conciseness** A satisfying or admirable neatness, ingenious
simplicity, or precision in something.

Even with these definitions, it's still hard to put your finger on
exactly what elegance is. Yet somehow, when you are in the midst
of it, you know. You walk into homes that reek with elegance.
You watch a deer jump over a fence. There is an elegance in
style and you know it when you see it, but to try to put it into
words is difficult. Someone comes up with an elegant solution

to a problem—an ingenious, simple solution. It's unique, special, simple, and *elegant*.

I'm mentioning elegance in this book not just because I like it, but to expose you to a wonderful book, *In Pursuit of Elegance*, by Matthew May. I highly recommend the book, as it is not only *elegantly* written, but it will open your eyes to a new way of thinking. May emphasizes that "simplicity" and "less is more" are foundations for elegance. And I believe they are also foundations to great businesses, great works of art, athletics, and life itself.

There is a lot of talk about the law of attraction, but May's book could easily have been titled *The Law of Subtraction: Your Key To Elegance*. He talks about how most people tend to try to add to or make things more complicated when in fact they should be doing just the opposite and looking at what can be taken away or subtracted to make things simpler.

As May says, "By nature we tend to add when we should subtract, and act when we should stop and think… We need some way to consistently replace value-destroying complexity with value-creating simplicity… We need to know how to make room for more of what matters by eliminating what doesn't. We all reach for elegance at some level, and yet it so often exceeds our grasp."[92]

This advice can be used in so many areas of your life. In business, think about possibly reducing the number of products you sell. In your home, look at what you can get rid of (furniture, clothes, magazines). In writing, eliminate unnecessary words to make your message more concise. In your golf swing, eliminate unnecessary moves to make your swing more efficient, effortless, and more powerful. Same thing for tennis and most other sports—simplify. Why do you think when you watch professional athletes, it looks so simple and effortless? Like they are hardly trying? In life, eliminate things you don't like and make more room for what matters to you. Elegance: we all need more of it in our lives.

Another interesting topic that May discusses in his book is certainty and predictability:

> When you remove certainty and predictability, engagement and awareness rise. The concept of shared space makes that clear. The less stated something is, the more powerful it becomes. Uncertainty and ambiguity can create intrigue, which makes us slow down and think. We don't immediately see the symmetry and order we so desperately seek and that transfixes our attention, draws us in.[93]

May goes on to explain that we are curious by nature, and we all have a need to know. We want to know what's missing. It intrigues us. We want to solve the puzzle. He writes of Leonardo Da Vinci and Michelangelo:

> Da Vinci instructs artists to leave any preliminary sketch indeterminate precisely because "confused shapes arouse the mind."... Leaving something for us to guess at was a stroke of genius... Michelangelo perfected and made famous a technique pioneered by sculptor Donatello before him, called *non finito*, meaning unfinished or incomplete. A shallow relief style, *non finito* not only left sculptures seemingly unfinished, it made them appear deeper than they actually were...
>
> But neither Leonardo nor Michelangelo was the first to explore the concept of purposefully unfinished or ambiguous work. As the Zen philosophy took hold

in Japan during the twelfth and thirteenth centuries, Japanese art and philosophy began to reflect one of the fundamental Zen aesthetic themes, that of emptiness. In the Zen view, emptiness is a symbol of inexhaustible spirit. Silent pauses in music and theater, blank spaces in paintings, and even the restrained motion of the sublimely seductive geisha in refined tea ceremonies all take on a special significance because it is in states of temporary inactivity or quietude that Zen artists see as the very essence of creative energy. Because Zen Buddhists view the human spirit as by nature indefinable, the power of suggestion is exalted as the mark of a truly authentic creation. Finiteness is thought to be at odds with nature, implying stagnation, which is associated with the loss of life. The goal of the Zen artist is to convey the symmetrical harmony of nature through clearly asymmetrical and incomplete renderings; the effect is that those viewing the art supply the missing symmetry and thus participate in the act of creation.[94]

Find ways to make your life more elegant by the law of subtraction. What can be taken out or removed for the betterment of your life? Simplify. Get rid of that extra hitch in your golf swing. Get rid of that loop-de-loop you have with your forehand in tennis. Get some elegance in your life today. Start by cleaning a small section of your closet, a small section of your garage. Start small so it's not overwhelming. Make small, subtle *elegant* moves.

When you tour new homes or model homes, why is it they look so elegant? Because no one has had a chance yet to "de-elegantize" (my word) them with all their personal clutter and belongings. Focus on the law of subtraction. Each day bring a little more elegance into your life. And you can start now by spending twenty dollars and purchasing *The Pursuit Of Elegance*. The small investment will pay off big.

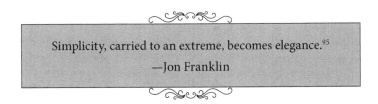

Simplicity, carried to an extreme, becomes elegance.[95]

—Jon Franklin

6

What Arises Subsides

As high as we have mounted in delight In our
dejection do we sink as low…[96]
—William Wordsworth

It's one of the greatest teachings or messages that the Buddha tried
to convey: that we all have the ability to recognize and be aware
that what arises also subsides. Every day, every moment, if you
remind yourself of this simple little truth, you will change the
way you view everything that happens during your day—good,
bad, or indifferent.

When I was younger, various things would inevitably come
up—in business or school, with friends or with family—that at the
time seemed to be so devastating, so traumatic, so heartbreaking.
I would feel I had reached a new level of low, and that life as I knew
it would never be quite the same again. It could be a bad grade on a
test, a bad performance in an athletic endeavor, an angry reaction
from my parents about something I did, a teacher upset with me,
my girlfriend breaking up with me… and then the next day, the
sun would come out, I would have gotten over my girlfriend and
met someone else, my teacher would let me retake the test, and

everything that had seemed so gloomy the day before would have taken on a whole new light. I was happy again. The gloom was gone. What arises subsides.

When bad things would happen to me, I would always react and overreact to whatever was happening. I bought into it as "real" and let it affect me and everyone who crossed my path, much like Jimmy Stewart's character of George Bailey in the movie *It's A Wonderful Life*. George becomes desperate and frantic when his uncle loses a big deposit. George is beside himself and takes it out on his family, friends, and everyone he encounters. He finally becomes so desperate he thinks he would be worth more dead (for the insurance money) than alive, and he attempts suicide. Most of you have probably seen this movie many times and know there is a happy ending to the story. George ultimately doesn't care about the money and realizes that his friends and family are what matter most in his life. His friends and family also rally to raise the money that was lost. It's a classic movie, but the point I am making is that as low as George had sunk when the money was lost, he rose to a height equally as high or higher when he realized his love for his family was all that really mattered. What arises subsides.

I remind myself of this saying all the time in business: What arises subsides. In business, there is always something going on that can take you on an emotional roller coaster. You lose a customer, an employee quits, you have to fire an employee, your competitors lower their prices to go after your customers, a truck breaks down, a customer files bankruptcy... almost every day there is some kind of mini-crisis in business. What I have learned from the Buddha and this simple saying is that it is only a crisis if you let it be. It's all how you react to whatever the major or minor crisis may be. You have complete power over your reactions and how they affect you. Knowing that what arises will also subside has had a profound effect on me, not only in business but also in life.

In most businesses, you are going to have a few occasions when a customer goes over to the "other side" and switches to a competitor. Fortunately, in our business, it hasn't happened a lot. At the time, you feel devastated, hurt, and frustrated. You never want to lose one of your customers. You start questioning what you may have done wrong. Was it customer service, product, pricing? Will we start losing more customers? Will we need to possibly lay off employees? All these thoughts run through your mind. You have trouble sleeping at night as you try to figure why the customer would leave. But if you understand what the Buddha was conveying in his simple message, you will have the wisdom to stop panicking and know that while it's never good to lose a customer, maybe something good will come out of it. Maybe you will become more aggressive at servicing your current customers. Thinking of ways to improve your customer service. Improve and become more efficient so you can possibly lower prices a little to keep your customers from looking elsewhere.

Just knowing that what arises subsides is comforting, because in almost all cases it holds true. The customer may come back to you because he or she didn't like the competitor's products and services. You may gain twice the business you lost because you were more focused and motivated to sell more. It may have been just the wake-up call you needed. You have new energy and focus. It stirs up the ego. Maybe you were resting on your laurels a little. Content. Satisfied. You needed the customer to leave (as bad as that may sound) to make you do something different. Suddenly the rain stops and the sun comes out. What you perceived as a disaster at the time turned out to be one of the best things that could have happened to your company. What had arisen has now subsided.

As the great Tibetan saint Patrul Rinpoche said,
"When your belly is full and the sun is shining upon you, you act like a holy person. But when negativities befall you, then you act very ordinary."[97]
—Anam Thubten

It's easy to be on top of the world when the sun is shining on you in life. But as soon as difficulties arise, you become very ordinary at best and probably hard to live with. You become absorbed in everything that's going against you. You are caught up in the moment and, without awareness, you let it ruin your day, week, or possibly your life. You don't realize that this awful circumstance will soon go away. As the saying goes, "This too will pass."

Virtually anything that might set you off: an argument with a friend, losing a customer, a cloudy or rainy day, a fight with a coworker, a comment someone makes to you, a fight with your spouse or children, a horrendous day on the golf course or the tennis courts, your car breaking down. Just when you think it can't get any worse, there is a break in the clouds and the sun peeks out. Your wife likes you again (for the time being), you give up on all the advice you've been given on your golf swing and start playing better, you start getting your serve in in your tennis match, and maybe your coworker starts talking to you again. How fitting is the song "What a Difference a Day Makes" or the saying "It's always darkest before dawn."

With thinking we may be beside ourselves in a sane sense. By a conscious effort of the mind we can stand aloof from actions and their consequences; and all things, good and bad, go by us like a torrent.[98]
—Henry David Thoreau

If it arises, it subsides. The good news is that we don't have to wait a day or a week, until dawn or until the sun comes out. Despite whatever is happening to you now (good or bad by your perception), you have the ability to recognize in this moment, to be aware in this moment that this condition that is arising will subside. Your ability to be aware of this universal truth is one of the most liberating and freeing actions that you can know.

It can change everything about your day and your life. You are no longer a prisoner of every little (or large) nuance that comes into your life. Things that used to bother you will no longer affect you. You may even chuckle at the drama that takes place because you know that it is just drama. It only affects you if you let it. You will still have moments and days in which you think that what has arisen will never subside. Even with this wisdom, there will be things that come up and make you say to yourself, "That arises/subsides stuff was nice, but it's not going to take care of this situation. I know what I am experiencing now will not subside. This is the exception to the Buddha's insight. The Buddha didn't know about this one. I have found the exception, and it is not good."

And at the time, it probably does feel that way. Nevertheless, it will, indeed, subside. As the saying goes, "Time heals all wounds." Maybe there are exceptions. If I lost one of my children, I am sure I would never fully recover. My life would never be the same as it was. But even though the pain from the loss of a loved one will never subside, most of our life encounters and situations that arise in our lives eventually do.

You are in a play called *Life*, and you are the director of your own play. You control how the scenes play out. You are still one of the characters in the play and can experience all the drama, but you are now in the director's chair and control how it affects you. You have all the power over your play and can change the script at any time. You are watching it unfold and yet still participating, as Thoreau said, with an "aloofness." And that is freedom.

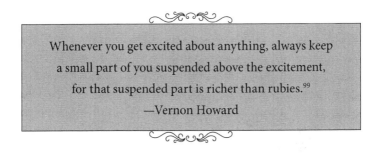

> Whenever you get excited about anything, always keep
> a small part of you suspended above the excitement,
> for that suspended part is richer than rubies.[99]
> —Vernon Howard

This topic is not just about the bad things that befall you, not just about the negative things that arise, but also the good things, the positive things and situations that arise. You may get promoted to a new position in your company, receive a pay raise, win your club championship in golf, win the lotto, do well on a test in school, and it may seem odd that you should keep some of your excitement at bay, as Vernon Howard suggests, when things are going really well for you. Being able to observe the excitement from a suspended state gives you the freedom of not becoming too attached to it, because it too will subside.

There's nothing wrong with basking in the glory and enjoying the rewards in the moment, but don't become consumed by it. You will have much better control over the way you react to all circumstances if you can be an observer as well as a participant in the good and bad in your life. That's the aloofness and suspended state that Thoreau and Vernon Howard were talking about. You will eventually become free of circumstances—good and bad.

What I mean by living to one's-self is living in the world, as in it, not of it… It is to be a silent spectator of the mighty scene of things;… to take a thoughtful, anxious interest in what is passing in the world, but not to feel the slightest inclination to make or meddle with it.[100]
—William Hazlitt

If you can incorporate this wisdom into your daily life, circumstances will never again affect you the way they once did. But the key is, you need to practice. You can't read this book once and expect to have mastered the concept. I practice every day or at least try to. I read and reread the teachings that are mentioned in this book as well as countless others on a daily basis, usually in the morning before I leave the house. Otherwise, it is far too easy to get caught up in daily activities and routines, reacting instead of watching and observing as a silent spectator. You quickly forget this valuable wisdom, and then you go through your day like a hockey goalie taking every puck (event) that is thrown at you and letting it affect you. You are led around like the cow in the busy Indian market by its nose.

Winter always turns to spring.[101]
—Taro Gold

A favorite story of mine is of the great Eastern philosopher, author, and guru Krishnamurti. An audience asked him what his key was to freedom and life. As they anxiously awaited the valuable insight from the revered master, he made this simple statement: "I don't mind what happens." Five words were the key to his life for freedom and happiness. Five words! His key to freedom was not getting caught up in the drama that can take place in our lives. He understood the simple message of "What arises subsides."

Things always arise in our household, as I am sure they do for you as well. It could be the roof leaking, children are sick, car breaks down, fender bender, forget to make a payment on one of your bills, lose your wallet, one of you kids fails a test. All of these things at the time can stir up all kinds of emotions, stress, and anxiety. Even though I have to deal with all of these issues—take care of them, fix them, do whatever it takes to make the situation better—I now have an aloofness about them. That doesn't mean that I ignore them and hope they go away, but I deal with them knowing that what may seem like a crisis is typically not as big as it's made out to be, and this too will subside.

I remember hearing Eckhart Tolle talking about spilling milk and saying, "Okay, I have spilled this glass of milk, and I now need to clean it up." He did not have thoughts like, *Great, why did this have to happen right now? I am in a hurry and this would happen. Why does this always happen to me?* It's almost as if he were watching the spilled milk from a suspended state but also recognizing that he would need to clean it up, without any emotions of it being good or bad. He just had to clean up the spilled milk.

If you can learn to incorporate this suspended state, this aloofness into your life, you will experience much less stress and worry. You will still accomplish the things you have always accomplished (and maybe more), and you will free yourself from getting too caught up in every circumstance that arises. You will be acting instead of reacting. The next time you are confronted with what you think is another major calamity, crisis, personal low, remember these three simple words: what arises subsides.

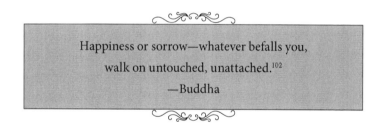

Happiness or sorrow—whatever befalls you,
walk on untouched, unattached.[102]
—Buddha

7

Why Thought?

Great men are they who see that spiritual is stronger than
any material force—that thoughts rule the world.[103]
—Ralph Waldo Emerson

I am including a chapter on "thought" because there is nothing in
our lives that will influence us more, whether we realize it or not.
All the great philosophers, spiritual teachers, and sages throughout
the ages have recognized the impact thoughts can have on our lives
and our well-being. No one can give an exact count on the number
of thoughts we have each and every day, but it is estimated at thirty
to sixty thousand. If you think about it (another thought), if we had
one thought every three seconds, that would equal thirty thousand
thoughts in a day, and that is probably a conservative number.

Thought is the key to all treasures.[104]
—Honoré de Balzac

So a better question would be: why not thought? Thoughts not only rule our world but also take us on wild, mental, and emotional rides. If you can harness the power of your thoughts, however, you can use them to your advantage. We don't have to get caught up in the mental drama that dominates our minds each and every day.

Most of us go through our entire lives without giving a whole lot of thought to thoughts. In school, we are taught math, science, biology, history, and English; we learn to memorize and solve problems, but at least in my case, not one teacher mentioned anything about our thoughts. My parents didn't discuss thoughts. My grandparents didn't. My doctors didn't. No one talked to me about thoughts. You accepted them for what they were, lived in a world of your five senses, and that's just the way life was.

Yet you and your thoughts go everywhere together. They are your best friend and your worst enemy. You are never without them. They can drive you insane, and they can take you to heights you've never experienced. They also have the power to imprison you for a lifetime. Nothing else in your life will have as much power and influence on you as your thoughts. Nothing will affect you more. Nothing is more important. Thoughts control every aspect of your life if you let them. And yet, they are rarely mentioned in schools, homes, churches, the doctor's office, or anywhere we look for enlightenment.

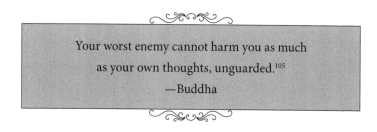

Your worst enemy cannot harm you as much
as your own thoughts, unguarded.[105]
—Buddha

Taro Gold, in his book *Living Wabi Sabi*, says this about your thoughts: "Nothing has caused you more trouble than your own psychology. Nothing has hurt you as much as your own thinking. Nothing is so frightening as the ideas that someone could read your mind! Pay attention to your thinking and you will see that 90 percent of your thoughts are fears, judgments, and worries. If you were to let these thoughts out onto the street, most of them would be arrested by lunchtime!"[106]

If you can master your thoughts, you can master your life. Behind thought lies the power of all creation. And this creation is not limited to new ideas and inventions. It extends to the creation of your life—how you view it, how you react to it, how you live it, and how your body and your mind respond to the nonstop bombardment of thoughts. If you let them, thoughts will rule your life and your world.

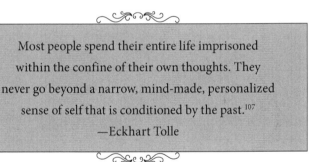

Most people spend their entire life imprisoned within the confine of their own thoughts. They never go beyond a narrow, mind-made, personalized sense of self that is conditioned by the past.[107]
—Eckhart Tolle

Thirty thousand thoughts a day can take you to many different places: happy, sad, overjoyed, depressed, lonely, scared, euphoric, worried, judgmental, enlightened… you can pretty much run the gamut on the wide variety of emotions and feelings that thoughts bring to your life each day. You may even experience all of the above feelings in one day! It's hard to believe you can go from depressed to euphoric to worried to overjoyed all in twenty-four hours, but it can and does happen.

And now for the bad news. Most of the thoughts you have are the same ones you had yesterday, and the day before that, and the day before that. Many of these are recurring thoughts that you have each and every day. Not only the same thoughts, but the same negative thoughts—the same fears, worries, and judgments—repeated day after day.

Since most of us have our daily routines, we are more likely to have the same kinds of thoughts each day, and it's very easy to focus on the negative ones. Maybe it's your dread of going to work, dealing with a coworker you have issues with, fighting the traffic to and from work (annoyed by all the bad drivers, even though you're never one of them), worrying about your children and their grades and getting them into college, fretting over bills you have to pay, strategizing things that need fixing in your home or apartment. You can dwell on and be consumed by all of these thoughts.

You could have a thought about one specific bill that you haven't paid, and just from thinking about this one isolated bill, your thoughts could go from where you will get the money to pay this bill to not having enough money to send your children to college. One minute you're thinking about a past-due cable bill, and the next minute your child may not go to college! And then worry and depression could set in.

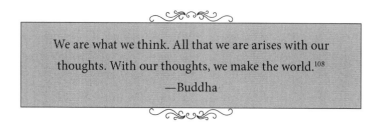

We are what we think. All that we are arises with our thoughts. With our thoughts, we make the world.[108]
—Buddha

In this case, the thoughts were financial, but they could be personal as well. Maybe it's something you don't like about yourself. Maybe you think you are too fat, too thin, too short, your nose is too big—and as you focus your attention on these thoughts, you help them grow, just like a seed. You are watering and fertilizing your negative thoughts. You are giving them power. And thanks to this power, they not only grow but come to control your life. The more you think about them, the more they will grow. But they are only as powerful as the attention you give them.

So we live in our own little thought world, engulfed in the same thoughts that we have every day (over and over) and even more engulfed by the negative ones. And the really bad news? You haven't given it a second thought!

> The one who learns how to control his thinking, learns how to control his destiny. We are bound by our own thought world. Nothing can save us but ourselves. The individual who will learn how consciously to change his thinking processes can remold his destiny.[109]
> —Ernest Holmes

In our lifetime, we could potentially have over a billion thoughts. Over a billion thoughts, and yet they are never discussed in school unless you happen to take some psychology or philosophy courses. We go through most of our lives with very little knowledge that we do have power over our thoughts. As Sakyong Mipham writes in his book *Ruling Your World*: "We let thoughts drag us around by a ring in our nose as if we were cows in an Indian market place. This is how we lose control of our lives. We live life in an anxious, haphazard state."[110]

In his book *The Untethered Soul*, Michael Singer describes such a state:

> "Did you turn off the lights downstairs? You better go check. Not now, I'll do it later. I want to finish watching the show. No, do it now. That's why the electric bill is so high."
>
> You sit in silent awe, watching all of this. Then, a few seconds later, your couch-mate is engaged in another dispute:
>
> "Hey, I want to get something to eat! I'm craving some pizza. No, you can't have pizza now; it's too far to drive. But I'm hungry. When will I get to eat?"
>
> To your amazement, these neurotic bursts of conflicting dialogue just keep going on and on… The bottom line is undeniable: If somehow that voice managed to manifest in a body outside of you, and you had to take it with you everywhere you went, you wouldn't last a day. If somebody were to ask you what your new friend is like, you'd say, "This is one seriously disturbed person. Just look up neurosis in the dictionary and you'll get the picture."[111]

Wherever the thoughts want to take us, we oblige and go along for the ride. And what a ride it can be! One minute you're on a roll with life, having nothing but good thoughts, and then you get a call from a creditor, someone cuts you off in traffic, you start worrying about saving money for retirement, you play over and over something somebody said to you or perhaps that you said to them, and pretty soon those good times you were experiencing a few minutes earlier are a distant memory. In a matter of minutes, you have gone from an emotional high to an emotional low, all because you let your thoughts drag you wherever they wanted to.

> Mastery of self-control of your thoughts and feelings is your highest achievement.[112]
> —Neville Goddard

Thoughts can affect every aspect of your life, including your health. I remember hearing Deepak Chopra recount that when patients were told they had cancer, they could age twenty years right in front of his eyes. A few seconds earlier they were fine. It's amazing, the power of just a few words spoken (nothing more than vibrations in the air). They can affect your entire physiology.

Think about a time when you were given bad news—maybe you lost a loved one, your boss fired you, your spouse announced an intention to leave you, someone told you that you were fat, ugly, stupid, any kind of negative news or negative remark—and think about how you felt. At the moment, even though you may not have realized it, you probably aged ten or twenty years. Not that it lasted, but in that moment, if someone had taken a picture of you, you probably wouldn't recognize the person in the picture.

That's the impact thoughts can have on you. And obviously, when thoughts get completely out of control, that's when people seek professional help. If you continue to be absorbed by negative thoughts, it can be the source of all kinds of disease. Negative thoughts can affect virtually every cell in your body, and not in a good way.

One of the hardest lessons we have to learn is that we build our bodies by our thoughts; that they are discordant or harmonious, diseased or healthy, in accordance with our habitual thoughts and the thought of those who preceded us.

There are those who, having learned this lesson, have had their countenance so altered in a single year by persistent right thinking, that one would scarcely recognize them. They have changed faces that were lined with doubt, disfigured with fear and anxiety, and scarred by worry or vice, to reflectors of hope, cheer, and joy.

Saint Paul showed scientific knowledge when he said: *Be ye transformed by the renewing of your mind.* That is, the changing, ennobling, purifying, refreshing of our thoughts. Growth everywhere neutralizes decay, renewing the mind. There is a law of perpetual renewal, a recreation constantly going on in us which is only interfered with by our adverse thought and discordant mental attitude.[113]

—Orison Swett Marden

If you only study one thing out of this entire book on a daily basis, I would probably recommend the passage above by Orison Swett Marden. That's the good news about thoughts. If we know that we have power over our thoughts and fully realize and utilize this power to our advantage, we can literally renew ourselves each and every day. We can stop the decay. We can grow. We can recreate ourselves now. Life is all about renewal—perpetual renewal. We are on a never-ending quest for renewal. It doesn't matter what age you are, because after all, that too is just a thought.

> The uncontrolled, ungoverned use of thought and feeling has brought about all kinds of discord, sickness, and distress. Few, however, believe this, and keep going on and on continually creating by their ungoverned thought and desire, chaos in their worlds.[114]
>
> —Saint Germain

I am in no way implying you can stop thoughts from entering into your mind—good, bad, or indifferent. You have no power or control over what comes into your thought world. But you do have power over how thoughts affect you, over how you react to them. Let the discordant and adverse thoughts pass with no effect. Give them no power.

Life can be difficult enough at times without you piling on and latching on to negative thoughts. Talk about your own worst enemy! Embrace the good thoughts. Think constructively. Tell yourself how magnificent you are, that every aspect of your being is renewing itself. Growth is only achieved by these types of thoughts. Stop the decay. Why not try it? Do you have anything to lose, except maybe ill health, depression, unhappiness? If you can do this and practice this every day, you will be renewed.

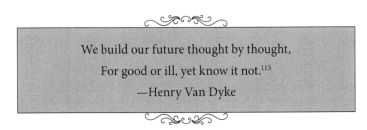

> We build our future thought by thought,
> For good or ill, yet know it not.[115]
> —Henry Van Dyke

I don't have any magic pills that will eliminate certain thoughts from entering into your brain—no one does—but I will tell you that you have an even more powerful weapon. You have the ultimate power in how you react to them. Thoughts are meaningless, passing in and out of your brain every few seconds, tempting you to latch on for a wild ride wherever they might be going (and usually no place good), but you don't have to latch on. They don't mean anything unless you give them meaning.

You have the power and ability to watch thoughts come into your mind, recognize them as just thoughts and nothing more, and let them depart with no side effects. No damage done. Rise above them and give them no credence. Be the watcher of your thoughts. Laugh at the ones that used to upset you. But grab on tightly to the good ones!

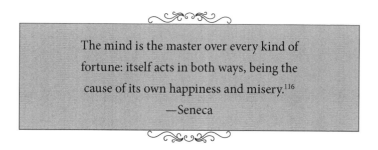

The mind is the master over every kind of
fortune: itself acts in both ways, being the
cause of its own happiness and misery.[116]
—Seneca

This ability to choose how you react to your thoughts is one of the most freeing and powerful tools you have in your life, and you need to use it. You need to embrace this power. Make it part of your daily ritual. Don't do it occasionally—do it every moment. It's not discussed in school because it's not part of the core curriculum and may be considered too mystical, too metaphysical, with not enough science behind it. So we let these thirty thousand thoughts drag us around because that's the way life is. We don't know any different. We are ignorant about thoughts. As Henry David Thoreau said, "With thinking we may be beside ourselves in a sane sense. By a conscious effort of the mind we can stand aloof from actions and their consequences; and all things, good and bad, go by us like a torrent."[117] It's a topic that should be discussed in every chapter of this book as a reminder of how important it is to your life, your health, your wealth, your happiness, and your well-being.

It is strange that we so long failed to understand the wonderful power of thought, for it is taught by every religion and philosophy in the history of the world. Thought is the only reality; conditions are but the outward manifestation of thoughts; as thought changes, all conditions must change in order to be in harmony with their creator, which is thought.[118]
—Venice Bloodworth

If you have the power to affect every cell in your body by the way you think and the thoughts you give credence to, why would you choose anything but the highest, the best, the grandest, the noblest thoughts possible? If negative thoughts can impact cells in a negative manner, the positive ones will do just the opposite. Forget the negative ones. Let them come and go like leaves blowing in the wind. The greatest, most magnificent power we all have is that *we can think whatever we want*. Right now, you can think whatever you want! No one can take that away from you. No one can come inside your mind and tell you to stop thinking that way.

It is the grandest freedom of all. It's our ultimate power. And although most of us were not exposed to this growing up and even as adults, it's not too late to learn. Starting now, you can change yourself, renew yourself, and empower yourself. You can begin now to change your life by the way you think and the way you react to thoughts. Why not? What have you got to lose? Where has latching onto negative thoughts taken you except on a downward spiral?

Decree now, and say it meaningly: "From this moment forward, I will admit to my mind for mental consumption only those ideas and thoughts that heal, bless, inspire and strengthen me."[119]

—Anam Thubten

8

Time to Wake Up

The awakened mind does not suffer from anything.
—Vernon Howard

Now that you have a better understanding of thoughts and how they can rule (and ruin) your life if you let them, it is appropriate to talk about waking up and bringing awareness into your life. Thoughts can only affect you if you allow them to. It's entirely up to you. You may not be able to control what thoughts come into your mind, but you certainly have the master key in how you let them affect you. If you rise above them and see them as just thoughts, watch them come and go without latching on to them, that is awareness.

Awareness has been taught by all the great spiritual teachers and sages throughout the ages. Most of us go through our entire lives without really knowing why things happen the way they do, why we are always the victim, why things never work out, why we always feel so down and angry, why we're always broke and unhappy, why we let every little thing that life throws our way affect us. *Why me?* We accept it as our fate in life, our calling in life, and we continue on our journey of misery. We buy into "that's just the way life is for me."

> The only true and full awareness is awareness
> of awareness. Till awareness is awareness
> of itself, it knows no peace at all.
> —Sri Ramana Maharshi

Awareness is the key to your freedom. Knowing that you know why something might be affecting you—that's waking up. That's awareness. Knowing that you have let your thoughts take you on an unnecessary journey down a dead-end path that only leads to misery, being conscious of this fact, and knowing that you can change your thinking and reactions at any time—that's awareness. You know these are just thoughts and that you have complete control over how they affect you. Your senses aren't always the reality. You can rise above all your thoughts and external environment and see them any way you want, on a daily, moment-to-moment basis. That's awareness, and it's your ticket to freedom, happiness, and bliss.

Awareness can be a very simple thing, and also can be extremely complicated. It's simple when you practice and incorporate it into every aspect of your life—not occasionally, but each and every day. It can be extremely hard if you don't think you have time, if you believe it probably won't work for you, that it's a little too "out there." You can be driving to work and as soon as someone cuts you off, you fall back into your old ways of reacting. You get mad and may want to retaliate. With awareness, you can watch your thoughts as they go down this path that leads to no place good. You can catch yourself and "see" yourself caught up in this moment of anger and let it go.

Or maybe when you get to work and you see an e-mail that upsets you, your blood pressure rises, and you want to react and respond immediately. You want to vent your anger, and without thinking you send off an e-mail that you later regret. With awareness, you can watch yourself get caught up in this little drama that has upset you and realize that there is no need to respond quickly and without thought. You can take your time, understanding that whatever has set you off is probably not that big of a deal, and you can either respond or not respond at a later time. That is awareness. You can actually "see" yourself getting angry, getting mad, wanting to retaliate. You may even find it humorous. How could something so seemingly benign affect you that way?

It can be hard, though, when you get caught up in daily life, with all the things that we have to do: going to the store, driving, going to work, school, social functions… In no time, you are back to being the person you have always been, reacting to life the way you always have. That's *unawareness*. That's living a life reacting to your senses, to your surroundings, to your environment. And that's how you lose control of your life, happiness, and freedom.

But if you practice awareness, if you start now (no better time than now), each day you will become more aware. Awareness will begin to become second nature to you. It is so important to make awareness, "waking up," a part of your daily life. In his book *A New Design for Living*, Ernest Holmes writes, "Man as a self-conscious expression of Spirit, which is never limited, encounters limitations only through his own thinking. Man imposes limitations on himself through wrong thinking. We must wake up to the tremendous creative nature of our thought. We can specifically, definitely, direct our thinking in such a way as to be productive of good in our experience."[120]

Learning how to harness your mind to promote *growth* is the secret of life, which is why I called this book *The Biology of Belief.* Of course the secret of life is not a secret at all. Teachers like Buddha and Jesus have been telling us the same story for millennia. Now science is pointing in the same direction. It is not our genes but our beliefs that control our lives… Oh ye of little belief![121]

—Bruce Lipton

Haven't you lived by your senses and same old reactions that have always plagued you for long enough? Don't you think it's time to try something different? Where has this type of living and thinking taken you? Do you like being dragged around by your thoughts, your environment—and even worse, someone else's thoughts, opinions, and advice?

There's an old story about a shaman with a reputation for curing insomnia. A busy professional who can't sleep tracks him down deep in the jungle, and the shaman agrees to help. The shaman sends instructions, and two weeks later, the professional sends back word that he's been cured. "Thanks so much! I've been sleeping great!" the note reads. The shaman sends back his own reply: "No problem. Come back and see me whenever you're ready to wake up."[122]

—Chris Guillebeau

Life and the concept of "me" is often described by many spiritual teachers as being similar to the ocean and the waves. We are much like the individual waves in the ocean that rise up and subside. The problem being that "we," as the waves, see ourselves as separate from the ocean, and when any little flare-up or disturbance comes our way, we believe it is exclusive to us. Any storm that comes along is "my" storm, "my" hurricane, "my" tsunami. We forget that we are the ocean. We forget that we are life. We forget that we are not separate from life, just as the wave is not separate from the ocean.

And yet we continue to go through life feeling we are separate, and consequently we go through life unaware. Even though you may think that you are aware, you probably are not. As Vernon Howard writes, "What is the condition of the unaware man? He does not know that he does not know. He is unaware, and so he is unaware that he is unaware. And being lost, he gullibly gives other lost people an opportunity to make him even more lost."[123]

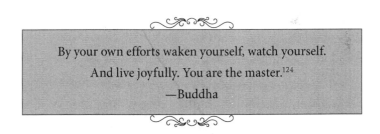

By your own efforts waken yourself, watch yourself.
And live joyfully. You are the master.[124]
—Buddha

I have lived the majority of my life unaware. And I was definitely unaware that I was unaware. I lived and reacted to what was going on around me, my senses, with no idea I had any control over how I reacted or how things external to me affected me. The entire time I was in control and yet I wasn't, because I didn't have this wisdom. I didn't know about these teachings.

In business, things are always popping up that, at the time, seem to be monumental. You lose a customer, you have to fire an employee, you receive an angry e-mail from a customer, and without awareness, you get caught up in the moment and deal with the problem without really thinking it through. You are reacting and oftentimes overreacting. You allow events and other people to make you even more lost.

Most of us live this way. We are all lost to some extent, as Vernon Howard would say. He adds, "Declare to yourself, 'Nothing in life has any meaning except my aim to wake up, to see life as it really is. So whatever my daily duties, I will use every minute, every thought and every energy to achieve this aim.'"[125]

It's tragic when we allow others who are unaware the power over us to make us even more lost. But you don't have to let this happen. You can wake up. You can become aware. And as you do become more aware, you will feel a great sense of liberation and freedom. You will start to see and understand your thoughts, your emotions, your up days, and your down days. You come to understand that what arises does subside. You start to realize there are no dualities in life, and the reason they existed before is because of the way you viewed and reacted to them. You viewed life on a sense level, letting everything that came your way affect you. You lived by your senses. You let outside circumstances control your life. You didn't create your life, you let your environment create you. You accepted this type of life as just the way life is. And that is the opposite of awareness.

> Self-awakening is the one great task of every man and woman on earth. To be self-awake is to be free of unconscious self-sleep. The first step toward Self-awakening is to detect one's actual state of psychic sleep, which is characterized by suffering, fear, anguish, and similar negative states.[126]
> —Vernon Howard

Many people use the popular expression, "It is what it is." But it doesn't have to be what it is. With awareness, you can change all of this. Don't buy into "It is what it is." You have complete control over the way you let any circumstance, event, anything external to you affect you. You are the conductor, the artist, the director, the painter, the sculptor of your life. What if Michelangelo had looked at the ceiling of the Sistine Chapel before he began his masterpiece and said, "Sorry, it is what it is"? Or looked at an uncarved block of stone and said, "Nothing I can do—it is what it is."

IT IS WHAT IT IS ° ° °

It is time to wake up and fully realize this wonderful power that we all have. The power of our thoughts and the power of awareness are two of the greatest powers any of us possess. Jesus tried many times to convey this simple message, telling us that "the kingdom of God is within you" (Luke 17:21). You have the kingdom of God in you now. It exists now. Jesus was telling us to wake up to this power within, and yet so few of us realize or know we have it.

> The millions are awake enough for physical labor; but only one in a million is awake enough for effective intellectual exertion, only one in a hundred million to a poetic or divine life. To be awake is to be alive... We must learn to reawaken and keep ourselves awake, not by mechanical aids, but by an infinite expectation of the dawn.[127]
> —Henry David Thoreau

Most of us tend to think that money and financial security will give us the freedom we want. It may help, but it's not lasting. You'll feel secure for a while, but that's not the security and happiness you're looking for. The real security is the knowing that you have the freedom to think anything you want, to believe anything you want, to react however you want to anything that arises, and to observe situations as though you were elevated above them and seeing them for what they really are. All of this comes from awareness. It comes from waking up from the nightmare that many of us live in on a daily basis—living like the hockey goalie of life, reacting, overreacting, and believing in every puck (life event) that comes our way.

Practice your new awareness every day. When you are in situations and can feel your blood pressure starting to rise because of what is happening around you, catch yourself before you get caught up in the melee of the moment and watch yourself become aware that you are aware. You can still deal with whatever is happening, but now you are dealing with the situation with awareness. You are not just reacting—or worse, overreacting. You elevate yourself to a higher level and see the situation much more clearly and calmly. And there is great power in that.

Hope is the dream of a soul awake.[128]
—French Proverb

The true freedom you are looking for is the freedom that we all have access to now. It is the heaven within. What could be more freeing than to be able to interpret and perceive life in any manner that we want, and to allow any thoughts to pass through like a leaf on a windy day, like a passing train? The thought could be as benign as a leaf or make as much noise as a train. But with awareness, you can silently watch them come and go. If you like one, grab onto it if it makes you feel better, if it empowers you. Relish it. You have the power to do whatever you want with it. But most importantly, don't let it adversely affect you. Don't buy into anything negative. Let those thoughts go. Learn to laugh at them.

What good comes from negative thinking? How can a negative thought possibly help you? Believing in a thought that has potentially dangerous and negative connotations can affect not only your mental well-being but also your physical well-being.

Maybe a thought pops into your head of something that has happened in the past, something you didn't like. Perhaps it was a negative comment, a situation or event that you wish hadn't happened, something you said that you wish you could take back. It could be anything, and when you replay it in your mind, all the old memories, frustrations, anger, guilt, all of the old emotions that you already once lived and suffered through come back to you, and you start reliving them again. You start tormenting yourself over something that may have happened yesterday or ten years ago. It instantly affects your mood and how you feel in the present moment, and you aren't even aware that you are doing this.

With awareness, you can let the thoughts, the old memories, come and go—no damage done. That is power! Awareness brings this to your life. It's your kingdom of heaven, the pot of gold at the end of the rainbow. It's the key to life. So wake up, bring awareness into your life, and you will forever change the way you view life.

You can develop the right mental attitude when you realize that nothing external can upset you or hurt you without your mental consent. You are the only thinker in your world; consequently, nothing can move you to anger, grief, or sorrow without your mental consent. The suggestions that come to you from the outside have no power whatsoever, except that you permit them to move you in thought negatively. Realize that you are the master of your thought-world. Emotions follow thought; hence, you are supreme in your own orbit...

You can voluntarily and definitely change your attitude toward life and all things. You can become master of your fate and captain of your soul...

Decree now, and say it meaningly: "From this moment forward, I will admit to my mind for mental consumption only those ideas and thoughts that heal, bless, inspire, and strengthen me.[129]

—Dr. Joseph Murphy

I will leave you with the title of Anthony Robbins's classic book, which sums up this chapter: *Awaken the Giant Within*! And by the way—that giant is *you*.

Over the years of traveling around and speaking with people, I have seen that there is clearly a deep, strong, and true desire to 'wake up,' whatever that means to any particular individual. There is a strong desire to realize God, to realize truth, to stop the violence, to stop the hatred, to stop the suffering and to wake up to what is possible in this lifetime.

If you want to awaken one hundred percent, If that has priority over everything else, then immediately you are awake. That's the truth. I stake my life on it. My life is guaranteeing that if you want to awaken to your true nature, if you want that totally, you will awaken to your true nature.[130]

—David R. Hawkins

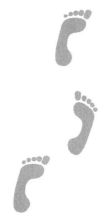

9

The Beauty of Rock Bottom

The highest condition takes rise in the lowest.[131]
—Publilius Syrus

The beauty of rock bottom? How can there be any beauty in hitting rock bottom? Though it seems illogical, hitting rock bottom may actually be one of the best things to happen to you in your life. It is that time when you are so far down that there's nowhere to go but up. We have all been there to some degree. It could be rock bottom in your finances, marriage, athletics, school, or physical health and well-being. It's that period in your life where you may even wonder if it is worth living.

I'm not talking about something like the loss of a loved one—that is a different type of rock bottom that everyone has to deal with in his or her own way. The rock bottom I will discuss are those times in your life where it seems as though you can't go any lower and something has to change; the times in your life when you are literally forced to change your life or you may end up being the loved one your family members are grieving over. It also doesn't have to be life-threatening, as you will see in some of my personal rock bottoms. Hopefully, if and when you find yourself in your personal rock-bottom state, you will use it as a wake-up call to do something different—to change something, to use it to your advantage. And if you do, that's where the beauty is.

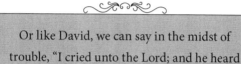

> Or like David, we can say in the midst of trouble, "I cried unto the Lord; and he heard me and delivered me out of my distress."[132]
> —Fenwicke L. Holmes

If you do hit this low point in your life, your personal rock bottom, something strange can happen. A sense of calm can come over you. It's a liberating calm. It's a powerful calm. You feel like finally you have nothing to lose. What used to seem like a really big deal is no longer that important. *I am at the lowest point in my life*, you think. *How could it get any worse?* If and when you find yourself in this dreaded condition, it may be the turning point that you were looking and longing for in your life. You needed to reach these depths so you can make a change. If you are halfway to rock bottom, you are less likely to change anything. Being halfway to rock bottom is pseudo-rock-bottom. Not quite bad enough to do something different.

> Some of us never quite come to ourselves in fullness and power until driven to desperation. It is when we are shipwrecked like Robinson Crusoe upon an island, with nothing but our own brain and hands, nothing but resources locked up deep in ourselves, that we really come to complete self-discovery. A captain never knows what is in his men until they have been tested by a gale at sea which threatens shipwreck.[133]
> —Orison Swett Marden

An example of pseudo-rock-bottom might be someone who is addicted to cocaine but can still manage to keep a job and a home despite being on the verge of rock bottom. People like that may be able to do just enough to get by and support their habit, but their habit has not yet ruined their life. They are teetering on the brink of rock bottom but not close enough to change what they are doing. And that's not a good place to be.

Halfway to rock bottom can be much worse than actually bottoming out. Halfway can lead to no change, not doing anything, just continuing on a destructive path. Once you find yourself truly at the bottom, that's when you know that something has to change. There is finally an awakening, a realization that you can't go on doing what you have been doing.

There could even be a feeling of freedom and liberation that you have never experienced. You feel empowered. It doesn't matter what happens to you now, what people think of you, what happens in your job (if you still have one), in your marriage (if you still have one), in your tennis game if you just lost your first set 6-0—it all doesn't matter, because you have hit rock bottom and it can't get any worse. That is very freeing.

There are two paths you can take when and if you hit rock bottom. You can decide to make a change and climb out of the hole, or you can stay right where you are. Many people do take this latter path. They give up on life, convince themselves that it's no longer worth living, and ultimately may even take their life or someone else's. They may resort to crime and end up in prison, or possibly homeless and living on the streets. This is not the beauty that I am talking about in this chapter. This chapter is about using rock bottom to your advantage. Using it as your wake-up call. Using it to change your life for the better. Using it to finally free yourself.

> At the depths of despair, nothing matters. I can't do anything, got to get out of here, walls falling in, throw me a rope, I can't move, can't stand it, throw me a rope... And one day, like any other day, finally tired of waiting for help that never comes, make a rope, tie it to a rock, throw it up, pull yourself out and walk away...[134]
> —Paul Williams

I remember times in my life when I felt I had hit rock bottom, and after the initial pain and shock, suddenly I felt like I could do anything I wanted. I knew I had to change what I was doing. Anytime you hit rock bottom, you can assume that whatever you have been doing in the past is not working. Albert Einstein is said to have defined insanity as "doing the same the thing over and over again and expecting different results."[135] We all do it. We're all insane to some extent. It's not easy breaking habits. It's too easy to be the "usual you."

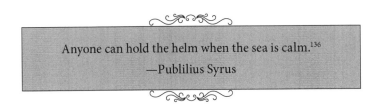

Anyone can hold the helm when the sea is calm.[136]
—Publilius Syrus

Most people tend to think of rock bottom as some type of financial crisis, and it could be. Maybe it's an addiction to alcohol, drugs, or gambling. You read in the paper or in the tabloids all the time about famous people who have checked themselves into rehab or therapy. Why? Because they have hit rock bottom. Even though they were on top of the world for a while, now they're at the bottom.

Look at Tiger Woods, one person who you wouldn't think could ever hit rock bottom. He probably hit it when his infidelity was exposed to the world. He could either continue what he was doing or make a change. By all appearances, it seems he chose change.

Tiger Woods, along with rock stars, movie stars, athletes, artists, and yes, even you and I—we've all had our personal rock bottoms. No one is immune. It's your wake-up call, and hopefully you're alert enough to hear the alarm clock. For me, it's as though rock bottom was exactly what I needed at exactly the right time. It was finally my chance to liberate myself from myself (the "usual me") and the life I was living. To make a change, I needed rock bottom.

> When you get into a tight place and everything goes against you, till it seems as though you could not hang on a minute longer, never give up then, for that is just the place and time that the tide will turn.[137]
> —Harriet Beecher Stowe

I will give you a couple of extremely mild examples of rock bottom in my life to show you that it doesn't have to involve drugs or alcohol, financial ruin, or the loss of a loved one. The concept is the same. These examples are in no way the worst rock bottoms in my life, as most of us would rather not share what our personal rock bottoms were. I use sports-related rock bottoms because whether it's sports-related, financial, marital, or drug- or alcohol-related, rock bottom means you need to change what you're doing.

One of my athletic rock bottoms came in the game of golf. I had been an avid golfer since I was six or seven, and at one time I had a handicap of around four or five. But as I became more involved in my business (finally realizing I could make more money in business than golf), I didn't practice golf as much. Yet I still felt I should be playing at the level I used to. I developed the "yips" in my putting stroke, and I couldn't make a two-foot putt. It was disastrous.

I'm sure you're thinking, "That's rock bottom?" Like I said, I've had much worse in my life, but if you're a golfer and you can't make a two-foot putt (not even close), yes, that's rock bottom for golf. I had never been that low in the game of golf—so I quit. That's right, I quit. No more golf. I had hit rock bottom. I knew I had to change something, so I took up tennis.

> Along your *Journey to the Impossible*, inevitably you are going to go through those times when you feel like there's no place left to go. Do this: Get excited! What? That's right; get excited because the unimaginable is about to happen. There are two options when caught between a rock and a hard place. You can *move the rock* or *blow through the hard place*. That's it. The above strategies are the keys to your doorway to the *impossible life*.[138]
>
> —Scott Jeffrey

And then I fell in love with tennis. I had always liked tennis and was a huge John McEnroe fan. My wife and I attend the US Open in New York every year, and tennis became my new passion. I became consumed by the game. I hit with the pro at our club at least four or five times a week for a minimum of an hour and a half. I was fascinated and possessed.

At first it was just for the exercise, as the pro would run me all over the tennis court and it was a great way to stay in shape. It didn't take four or five hours like golf, and it was more fun than running. It was a nice break from golf. As I practiced religiously almost every day, I started to get better, so I decided to test my skills in some tournaments.

I didn't fare very well in my first few tournaments, but as time went on, my game continued to improve. For me, a high point was winning the club 4.0 tennis tournament, which for you tennis fans out there is not like winning the city open, but not bad for someone who had not been in the game that long. For you non-tennis fans, there are many levels of tennis, starting at 2.5 and going up to 6.0 or 7.0 and then the professional ranks.

> True freedom is the loss of everything. Because you have nothing, there is nothing to lose. This is the end of fear.[139]
> —Jeff Foster

The reason I am telling you this is not to bore you with my mediocre tennis accomplishments, but to point out that rock bottom in golf led to something completely different that was exactly what I needed. As I played more and more tennis, becoming even more consumed by the game, my competitiveness also was on the rise. At first, being competitive was just part of the game. But I was now taking it to another level, and that's not always a good thing.

I started worrying about players that I "should beat." There is no harder opponent in tennis than the one that you "should beat." The game wasn't as much fun as it used to be when I was just playing for exercise. I still loved tennis, but my competitive side was beginning to be more important than the game itself.

My rock bottom came when I was skiing with my wife and young daughter and, as we were skiing on a "cat track," my daughter went between my legs for fun, closed her eyes, and headed straight down. You may not be a skier, but imagine doing the "splits" on skis. The pain was excruciating. Not long after the skiing accident, the pain I thought was from a groin pull actually turned out to be hip problems that were exacerbated by the skiing accident.

Now that you seemed to have lost something (possibly everything), hopefully you've learned to trust and surrender. In so doing, you probably are open to new ideas and inspirations, all of which are leading you to the potential of creating *A New Life*.[140]
—Michael Mirdad

To make a long story short, I ended up having arthroscopic hip surgery the next two years on both hips, effectively putting my tennis game on hold for a few years. Because tennis had been my passion and love for the past five or six years, this seemed like another rock bottom. Because I wasn't able to play tennis for a few years, I knew I had to change something in my life, so I began to read more. As much as I hate to say it, I actually needed this break from tennis, because I was becoming too competitive and I needed a wake-up call.

How sickness enlarges the dimensions of a man's self to himself![141]
—Charles Lamb

If I had not had the accident and the surgeries, I might never have found my new passion for reading and studying the topics discussed in this book. It's been *by far* the best thing that has happened in my life. Life takes some strange twists and turns, but most of them are for the better. You just have to be awake enough to realize it.

> In extreme timeless agony, the soul may entreat, "If there is a God, I ask him for help," and a great transformation occurs. This confirms the truth of the Zen teaching, "Heaven and hell are only one-tenth of an inch apart."[142]
> —David R. Hawkins

These extremely mild rock bottoms I've described are similar to major rock bottoms in that they almost always lead to something greater if you decide to make a change. No matter what level of rock bottom I've experienced in my life, there has always been a feeling of empowerment, freedom, and even relief afterward.

The Roman satirical poet Juvenal is quoted as saying, "The man whose purse is empty can cheerfully sing before the robber."[143] When you have nothing to lose, you have nothing to give a robber, and you are not affected by this particular misfortune. I'll use tennis again as an example. As an avid tennis fan, I can't count the number of times I have seen a player lose the first set 6-0, which in tennis is also known as a *bagel*. You can't get a worse score for one set in tennis. You have hit rock bottom in tennis games, and at this point, you have nothing to lose. You have been humiliated, and it would seem like there would not be much hope for the second set. But it's actually shocking the number of times the player who has just been "bageled" in the first set comes back and wins the second—not only wins, but many times beats the opponent by the exact same 6-0. Believe me, this is not that uncommon.

What's the reason for this remarkable turnaround? It's because you hit rock bottom and now you can start going for it. You can play the game like you know how to play it instead of playing not to lose. You cannot possibly do worse. You are more relaxed, the tension is gone, you go for your shots, and good things start to happen. You have hit rock bottom and you are climbing out of your hole with everything you can muster. You no longer look or act like the same scared, weak, intimidated player who was humiliated in the first set. You are confident, carefree, and driven, all because you hit rock bottom. There is beauty in that!

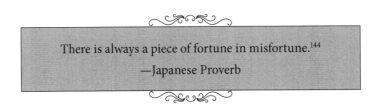

There is always a piece of fortune in misfortune.[144]
—Japanese Proverb

The same goes for golf. For you golfers out there, how many times have you just had your worst hole, only to follow it up with a birdie or par on the very next hole? It happens all the time. Or in match play, when one player is down three with three holes left to play and comes back to actually win the match. The pressure the opponent initially may have felt is gone, and with his or her back against the wall, the player makes a dramatic comeback. The opponent can "sing before the robber," because what is there to lose at that point?

The same goes for other areas of life. You finally get your wake-up call. You're no longer going to drive yourself insane by doing the same thing every day. You're at your wits' end, and you have to make a change. You take the attitude, "At this point, who cares?" You forget about any kind of outcome and go for it. There is nothing to lose by making a change, because you know where the "usual you" has taken you. Good things start to happen. You have a new laser-like focus on what you want to do and accomplish.

You have a carefree attitude, because you know things can't get any worse. You loosen up. You are more confident. You have empowered yourself to do something far different and far greater.

Far too often, most of us change only when we are faced with a crisis, trauma, or discouraging diagnosis of some sort. The crisis commonly comes in the form of a challenge, which may be *physical* (an accident, say, or an illness), *emotional* (the loss of someone we love, for example), *spiritual* (for instance, an accumulation of setbacks that has us questioning our worth and how the universe operates), or *financial* (a job loss, perhaps). Note, all of the above are about losing something.

Why wait for trauma or loss to occur and have your ego knocked off balance due to the negative emotional state? Clearly, when a calamity befalls you, you have to act—you can't take care of business as usual when you've been knocked, as the expression goes, to your knees.

At those critical moments when we've really, really grown tired of being beaten down by circumstances, we'll say; *This can't go on. I don't care what it takes or how I feel (body). I don't care how long it takes. No matter what's going on in my life, I'm going to change. I have to.*[145]

—Dr. Joe Dispenza

And as a side note for you golf fans, after basically quitting the game for a while, I did start playing golf again—the game that I grew up playing and love. A two-foot putt is not that big of a deal in the scope of life. After hitting rock bottom in golf and putting, I had to make a change, so I went to the "claw" in my putting stroke, and my yips are gone (for now). Nothing really bothers me anymore about my golf game because I have already experienced rock bottom.

A rock bottom is anything that forces you to change what you have been doing, to free yourself from yourself. If you have not hit rock bottom in your life, do as Dr. Joe Dispenza says: Don't wait for the trauma or loss to occur or for the calamity to befall you. Change now! Don't wait any longer. Experience the beauty of rock bottom without actually going there.

> When apparent adversity comes, be not cast down by it, but make the best of it, and always look forward for better things, for conditions more prosperous.[146]
> —Ralph Waldo Trine

This poem by Robert Browning Hamilton is a fitting end to "The Beauty of Rock Bottom":

> I walked a mile with Pleasure;
> She chatted all the way;
> But left me none the wiser
> For all she had to say.
>
> I walked a mile with Sorrow;
> And ne'er a word said she;
> But, oh! The things I learned from her,
> When Sorrow walked with me.[147]

10

Picture This

Through the manifestation of the power that is within you, you can
project any objective experience which you may legitimately desire.[148]
—Ernest Holmes

There is nothing more freeing than the exercise I am about to
describe to you. You may have a hard time believing or buying into
this message, but if you practice what I discuss on a daily basis and
have faith, you will be shocked by how it can transform your life.
What is this magical formula that is going to be so freeing and
life-changing? You are probably assuming it will be difficult if it
can have such a profound effect on your life. But it is one of the
easiest things in the world to do, if you do it each day and have
faith and belief in it.

Every sage, every prophet, all the great masters, Jesus—they
have all tried to convey this message to their listeners, and the
message is: you have the power in you every day to become the
perfect you, the idealized you, the greater you, the greatest you,
the you that can become anything that your mind can visualize
and that you can believe in. That the kingdom of heaven is within
and available to you at all times. If you can picture the ideal you

(whatever that may be) in your mind and see yourself being this person throughout your day, you will become that person.

Through your faculty to imagine the end result, you have control over any circumstance or condition. If you wish to bring about the realization of any wish, desire, or idea, form a mental picture of fulfillment in your mind; constantly imagine the reality of your desire. In this way you will actually compel it into being. What you imagine as true already exists in the next dimension of mind, and if you remain faithful to your ideal, it will one day objectify itself. The master architect within you will project on the screen of visibility what you impress on the mind.[149]

—Dr. Joseph Murphy

You are the master architect. So why not create a masterpiece? Being able to create any kind of reality you want, any kind of "you" that you want, is one of the greatest freedoms that we all have access to. The problem is, most of us don't know it. I only wish I had learned this many years ago. I used this power at times, but I was unaware that I was using it. It is one of the most liberating and inspiring things you can do, and yet most of us believe that we are dealt certain cards in life and can't change the hand we were dealt.

It's easy to fall into this trap. It's easy to believe this, because it gives you an excuse. It's a way to live below your capabilities, below your dreams, below expectations you have for yourself. It's too easy to not live up to what you might become. But my message to you is to rise up and create a new you. Forget the you that you think you are. Become someone far greater.

As Neville Goddard writes, "You are already that what you want to be but refuse to believe it."[150] We are unaware of this. We live by our senses, by appearances, by our environment. We accept what other people tell us. But what I am telling you can change that. You have the power to become what you already are, which is perfect. You need to wake up to this realization and start believing it. You form the picture on the inside and it manifests on the outside. Goddard also states that, "All of creation is finished—it is only to be manifested."[151] The perfection is in you now, but it needs to be manifested. The potential to go to the moon has always existed, automobiles, electricity, airplanes—creation is done. The manifestation is the only missing piece of the puzzle.

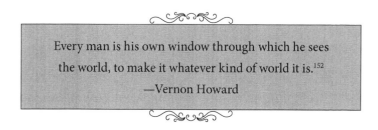

Every man is his own window through which he sees the world, to make it whatever kind of world it is.[152]
—Vernon Howard

I believe this is the greatest gift we all have: to make our world whatever kind of world we want. What could be more liberating? There is no better time to start your journey on this new path of manifesting your world than right now.

Try this for a few weeks, and you will want to do it the rest of your life: before you leave your house to start your day—and even if you don't leave your house—take ten minutes (or longer if you can) and create the perfect you. You may be thinking, *The 'perfect you'? What does that mean?* I'm not saying there is anything wrong with the *present* you, but it simply means the perfect, idealized conception of yourself that you would like to be. It can be anything you want. It can be a slimmer you, a more muscular you, a fatter you. Maybe there's an entertainer or an athlete who you admire and would like to be more like. It could be a you that is more confident and self-assured. It could be a happier you.

The "perfect you" is your own personal creation of whatever you want and see as being the ideal person you would like to be. You are the creator. This isn't about just thinking positive thoughts. It's about forming a mental picture in your mind of a new you, and throughout your day, acting, walking, talking, and behaving as if the new you actually exists *now*—not sometime in the future when you have lost the ten pounds you wanted to lose before you could be happy, or have taken some courses or read some books on how to be more confident, or have developed the skills that will turn you into a star athlete. The only time to do anything is now. Start practicing this now. Become the idealized and greater you now. Don't wait for an imaginary future day that never comes.

Picture your ideal in life; live with this ideal.
Let the ideal capture your imagination; Let the
ideal thrill you! You will move in the direction
of the ideal that governs your mind.[153]
—Dr. Joseph Murphy

You may be thinking, *This all sounds nice, but I just ate the last piece of cake this morning, I'm overweight, and I am not happy* about myself. *How can I possibly imagine being the perfect me now?* If that's the case, you can start right now by thinking, *I won't diet, but I will not eat quite as much today as I normally do. I won't have that extra helping that I normally have, and maybe I will skip the second helping of dessert tonight.* And if you don't exercise, start today and go out for a short walk. I'm not saying you need to join a health club, hire a trainer, run five miles—just do a little bit more exercise than you normally do. Walking is a great way to get outside and enjoy nature, and it's also great exercise. See yourself right now as becoming the more perfect you by taking small steps. Baby steps. The whole time, see yourself in your mind as being healthier and slimmer.

One thing I started doing each day when I first learned and was exposed to these teachings was to spend five to ten minutes each morning reading my favorite excerpts from books on these teachings. It only took five to ten minutes out of my day, and yet it had and still has a profound impact on how my day unfolds. I could be tired, not feeling great, lethargic, and after just ten minutes of reading my entire outlook would change as well as my physiology. I was no longer tired. I was excited about the day. I had renewed enthusiasm. Just five to ten minutes each day, and I was a new person. Those are the baby steps I am talking about— baby steps for everything you are trying to change and improve on. Whether it's exercising, eating a little less, reading, writing, practicing something new in your golf swing, playing the piano… take the baby steps now that will inspire you to an entirely new day, new life, new you.

Every day, create your day. Create yourself. Create your reality. Why not? Who is going to stop you? Do you think any of your coworkers, family, or friends can stop you? They may wonder why you seem so happy, so confident, so different, but they won't have access or control over what or how you think. They may think they do and perhaps would like to have control, but you are the master of your thought world. You have the power to think any thoughts you like, any thoughts that will benefit you.

Here is a simple formula. Take your attention from your present conception of yourself and place it on that ideal of yours, the ideal you had heretofore thought beyond your reach. Claim yourself to be your ideal, not as something that you will be in time, but as that which you are in the immediate present. Do this, and your present world of limitations will disintegrate as your new claim rises like the phoenix from its ashes.[154]
—Neville Goddard

You are probably still thinking, *Yeah, this all sounds great, but the minute I step out the door I will forget about the perfect me and go back to being the usual me. It sounded good when I was reading it, but I doubt if it will work for me because I have all these things that I have to deal with in life. I don't have time to try to be the perfect me while dealing with life, and it probably wouldn't work anyway. My schedule is too busy to try to create my reality. My present me and living by my senses hasn't been that bad. I seem to get through life okay and am relatively content.*

Maybe that's what you want, but I don't think you would have bought this book if you were content with your life the way it is now. Again, I'm not saying you need to make any drastic changes or that there is anything wrong with you now, but practicing some of these baby steps will have a profound effect on your life.

Forget appearances. That's not what this is about. The only thing that matters is what you picture in your mind. No one else lives in your mind. You can picture and think anything you want. All appearances are an illusion. They come and go but are never the same. So forget appearances except for the one you have in your mind. That's the only one that is important. This isn't about becoming something better in the future. It's about this moment. This moment you are slimmer. The scale may not reflect that at this moment, but your mind and your visualization do. Your job is to hold and picture that thought throughout the day and disregard all appearances and evidence to the contrary.

You may also be wondering what I mean by "appearances are an illusion." I will give you an example: You are standing in line at the supermarket, and while waiting, you scan the covers of several tabloids that are luring you to buy them and find out what the latest gossip is on your favorite celebrities. One tabloid has a famous actress on the front cover dressed in an evening gown, hair perfect, makeup perfect… and the tabloid right next to this one may have that same actress or celebrity on the cover with a headline like, "Famous celebrities without their make-up." That tabloid has a picture of this very same actress but without makeup and carefully styled hair, and you wonder if it is the same person.

I point this out not to say that one is better than the other, but to show that appearances are illusory. They come and go. Forget appearances. If you live by appearances, you are living by your five senses. There is a much greater way to live.

> Live your life in a sublime spirit of confidence
> and determination; disregard appearances,
> conditions, in fact all evidence of your senses
> that deny the fulfillment of your desire.[155]
> —Neville Goddard

So now you are probably thinking, *If I should forget appearances, why should I try to create the perfect me? Why should I try to become slimmer? More perfect?* And again, I want to emphasize that there is nothing wrong with the present you. You may be perfectly content. But most of us aspire to become better and greater. And if you believe in your mind that you are the perfect you, regardless of appearances, you will be more confident and have an aura about you that you didn't have before. You won't spend your day consumed by your weight or whatever you are consumed by.

If you practice the baby steps I am talking about, you will enjoy life more, your confidence will grow, and your whole demeanor will change. We can't help but live by appearances to some degree, but if you learn to live your life disregarding them, you will be happier. And if you still want to live by appearances, try to view everything you see as perfect. See perfection in everything. Once you start doing this, you will forget about appearances.

To give you an example of how powerful this concept is and how powerful our thoughts are, have you ever wondered how impersonators can instantly become someone else? They talk, walk, act, and actually look like whoever they are impersonating. Right before your eyes, they become that person. They transform themselves to become someone else. They manifest themselves into the person they are impersonating. How do they do this? Obviously it takes practice, but in their mind, they see themselves as being that person or thing. In their imagination, they are that person. Whatever is on the inside manifests itself on the outside. It's amazing to watch someone become somebody else right before your eyes.

I give you this example of an impersonator because whoever he or she is trying to impersonate, it all comes from within. Impersonators look and talk like someone else because of their thoughts and imagination (all from within), which then materializes on the outside. It manifests itself. That is what I'm talking about in creating and picturing the perfect you. It's from within—from your thinking and your thoughts.

The good news is, you don't have to be a professional impersonator to transform yourself and your life. I'm not great at impersonating because I don't practice it, but occasionally when I try to imitate someone else, I surprise myself by how much I actually sound like the person I am trying to imitate. I not only sound like that person but also take on his qualities. I begin to look and feel like the person I am impersonating. And it all comes from the mind—from thoughts, imagination, and belief that I am that person. Become the impersonator of your life and imagine yourself as whatever you would like to be. Who is going to stop you?

If you believe yourself to be an artist, then everything becomes possible again. Words are your paintbrush, and your life is the canvas. You can paint whatever you want to paint.[156]
—Don Miguel Ruiz and Don Jose Ruiz

The world is your oyster. Make it any kind of world you want. You are the creator of your life. You are the painter. You are the artist. And if you take my advice and the advice of all these great masters, you will paint a masterpiece. Picture in your mind what your masterpiece is and become it. Do it every day without fail.

As soon as the individual becomes aware that he really has control of his own Creative *thought, power,* and *feeling,* then he knows positively that he can precipitate into his visible use, or bring into his use from the outer where it is already created, *anything whatsoever* upon which he hold his Creative thought and feeling firmly.

The moment that he is truly aware of this, he will know he is forever free from the need of the wealth of the outer world, or anything that the outer world can give. Thus he has entered into the Mastery and Dominion of his world, the only world that is ever existent to him, and which is his God-given Birthright.[157]

—Saint Germain

Things to Ponder

PRAISE AND CRITICISM

You can't let praise or criticism get to you. It's a
weakness to get caught up in either one.[158]
—John Wooden

What's wrong with receiving and basking in a little praise? There
is nothing wrong with it. Praise can be constructive; it can help
motivate you. It can be an indicator of your performance. We like
it. We want more of it. We crave it. And we can also become a slave
to receiving it. We may need the praise to bolster our self-esteem,
to feel good about ourselves.

But you are not defined by praise, any more than you are
defined by criticism. You don't have to receive praise to feel good
about yourself or your performance. When you do rely on praise
to feel better about yourself, you may become a slave to what
someone else thinks. Below are some of my favorite quotes on
this topic.

There is no greater bane to friendship than
adulation, fawning, and flattery.[159]
—Marcus Cicero

Hear me now: Don't waste time listening to false praise
or distorted criticism. The praise will go straight to your
head and the criticism will go directly to your heart.[160]
—Pete Wilson

Whenever a man's friends begin to compliment
him about looking young, he may be sure
that they think he is growing old.[161]
—Washington Irving

As far as criticism is concerned, nothing good comes out of it. To criticize another? Who is so superior that he or she can be a critic of another human being? You may say, "What about constructive criticism?" And again I would say, no one has the right to criticize. Using the word "constructive" is just trying to soften the blow.

A basketball coach may point out to one of his players a constructive way to play defense, but he doesn't need to criticize the player for the way he currently plays defense. The same thing in business: if you are in a position of authority, you can point out what an employee did wrong and offer tips or advice on how to handle the situation next time, but you don't need to criticize. You don't need to offer the feared "constructive criticism."

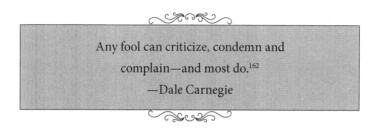

Any fool can criticize, condemn and
complain—and most do.[162]
—Dale Carnegie

The sages are trying to tell us not to get caught up in either praise or criticism, the good or the bad.

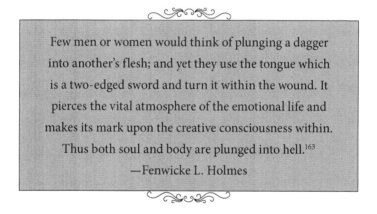

Few men or women would think of plunging a dagger
into another's flesh; and yet they use the tongue which
is a two-edged sword and turn it within the wound. It
pierces the vital atmosphere of the emotional life and
makes its mark upon the creative consciousness within.
Thus both soul and body are plunged into hell.[163]
—Fenwicke L. Holmes

You may not think when you are offering someone your opinion or even worse, criticism, that it could have the kind of effect that Fenwicke Holmes is describing—but it could. That's why you should never criticize. Be careful about your praise as well. Ask yourself: who am I to judge? The world is a mirror. That which you are criticizing is a reflection of you.

You have reached the pinnacle of success
as soon as you become uninterested in
money, compliments, or publicity.[164]
—Thomas Wolfe

ust as a solid rock is not shaken by the storm, even
so the wise are not affected by praise or blame.[165]
—Buddha

DON'T BE THE "USUAL YOU"

There is something in you that is capable
of not being the usual you.
—Vernon Howard

At this very moment, the majority of the population is maneuvering around the planet on cruise control. You wake up, start the day (your engine) in your typical fashion, drive down all the same roads, and as your head hits the pillow at night, if you have taken any time at all to reflect on your day, you will find that it was virtually identical to the day before. And not only the day before, but the day before that, and the day before that. You're cruising down the highway of life, giving very little thought to the fact that your life is just one big yesterday.

Maybe you wonder, *Why am I in such a rut? Why do things never change? Why do I still have this job I hate, live in this dumpy little house, have the same bills—and now some new ones to add to my existing ones? Why do I never have any money, still watch the same TV shows at night, have the same 30,000 thoughts that I had yesterday?* Yet you just let the cruise control take over and take you wherever it wants.

We all drive this same car of life, and yet so few know that you can turn the cruise control off, shift gears, put the car in reverse, and go in another direction. Somewhere exciting, to places that you have never been. Unfortunately, we are like robots that climb into this car of life and let it do the driving. You don't feel good about it. You know you need to do something different, but it seems like it is just too hard to change. It's far too easy to let the car of life take you on that same *Twilight Zone* trip that you take every day, and nothing ever changes.

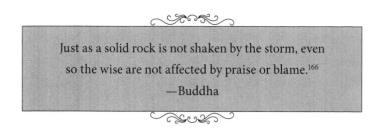

Just as a solid rock is not shaken by the storm, even so the wise are not affected by praise or blame.[166]
—Buddha

But fortunately, there is something you can do, and it is not difficult. Starting today, put your car and life in reverse. Do it now! Don't waste any more fuel on your current dead-end trip that takes you to the same dead-end places every day. You've wasted enough fuel, energy, time, potential. It doesn't matter what kind of car (life) you're driving now; it could be an old jalopy, a Ferrari, or anything in between. You may not have a penny to your name or you may have millions in the bank, but it doesn't matter if you are dissatisfied with your current cruise-control life—your usual you.

It's very easy to be the person you have always been, for it requires no change, no self-reflection and no growth.[167]
—Taro Gold

Not only can you reverse your life, but more importantly, you can also reverse your thoughts. What do I mean by reversing your thoughts? Let me give you an example. Instead of your typical Monday-morning thoughts of dreading the start of a new work week, dreading going to the office or wherever you work, dreading having to talk to the same coworkers and your boss, dreading all the things you typically dread—reverse all those thoughts. Reverse your thinking. As the Nike ad says, "Just Do It." What have you got to lose?

Look forward to going to work and maybe coming up with a new idea. Or look at your current job as a way to help you financially until you can do what you really want to do. Look at your current job as a means for you to pursue your real dream. Any negative thought that comes to mind, reverse it.

Let's say you typically wake up, head to the bathroom, grumble about how bad you look, complain that you don't have time for breakfast, observe that the weather is rainy, hear that the dogs are barking, and wish you could crawl back into bed. Just the usual you in action. But since you are now in control of your life, reverse all these thoughts. Tell yourself how great you look (if you do this enough, you might start believing it). Tell yourself to eat a healthy breakfast. Tell yourself how excited you are about your new outlook, your new possibilities, your new life! Reverse all those old, worn-out thoughts, and do it all day long.

Man's world of affairs is the result of his self-contemplation. He is, at first ignorant of this, and so binds himself through wrong ideation and action; reversing this thought will reverse the condition.[168]

—Ernest Holmes

On your drive to work, when the person talking on his cell phone cuts you off, instead of reacting or retaliating in your old angry or aggressive manner, reverse all of those reactionary thoughts that you normally would have. Change them to something like, *Isn't that amusing*, or smile and know that you no longer will react the way you used to. Feel sympathy for the person who cut you off, who most likely drives that way every day, in a continual state of having to get in front of the car in front. Know that such drivers are on a never-ending dead-end goal. Smile because you have read this book, and they most likely haven't! Try it for one day and see if it makes any difference in your day, in how you feel, in how you view life.

> What a tragedy to think this is the best we can do with
> our lives. We are not confined to the habitual path.
>
> —Vernon Howard

For those of you who remember the *Seinfeld* TV show, there was an episode in which George, who typically has annoying and bad things happen to him on a daily basis, decides to think and act in exactly the opposite manner he normally would. He reverses his usual George, his usual way of thinking and acting. He did the opposite. And sure enough, his life changed immensely for the better. He was offered a great job, women were attracted to him, every negative thing that typically happened to him suddenly turned positive and good fortune came his way. All because he decided to think and act in exactly the opposite way of his usual thinking and reacting. Doors opened and opportunities came about that never did before.

Even though this was just a sitcom and obviously not a true story, and George did go back to being the usual George, the message conveyed is the same message I am conveying to you. You can get out of your daily rut and routine, your daily way of thinking and reacting, the usual you, and put your life in reverse. Why not try it? What have you got to lose?

> When we reverse our attitudes about life, and accept all that's already good, true, and beautiful, we move into the have consciousness. That is when it will be proved to us that *nothing is too good to be true.*[169]
>
> —John Randolph Price

Put your life in reverse *now*! Stop being the usual you. Astonish yourself with your newfound good fortunes, because nothing is too good to be true.

FOR YOUR OWN GOOD

> The usual excuse of those who hurt others is
> that they do it for their own good.
> —Marquis de Vauvenargues

Have you heard this before? "It's for your own good." "I'm doing it for your own good." "They are only doing it for your own good." "We are just doing it for your own good." Who are these people who are doing something for "your" own good? Isn't it strange that "they" know what is good for you?

Understandably, parents (especially when their children are young) may have a right to make such a lofty proclamation. You would hope that most parents would know what is for the good of their children, but it usually doesn't stop there. You could be an adult and they may be still be telling you that they are doing something for your own good. Maybe you still need it, but let's hope not. And this "I am doing it for your own good" is not exclusive to your parents. Teachers, doctors, politicians, bankers, judges, bosses, coworkers, friends—virtually no one is excluded from this knowledgeable group that knows what's best for you, except maybe your children (and if they say it, you probably do need to listen).

As David Hawkins says in his book *Eye of the I*, "With humility comes the willingness to stop trying to control or change other people or life situations or events ostensibly 'for their own good.' To be a committed spiritual seeker it is necessary to relinquish the desire to be 'right' or of imaginary value to society."[170]

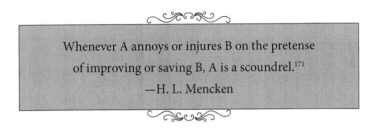

Whenever A annoys or injures B on the pretense
of improving or saving B, A is a scoundrel.[171]
—H. L. Mencken

There is no shortage of people out there who know what's best for you. People love to control other people's lives or situations. There is also a sense of power and control when you tell someone else that "you" are doing something for "their" own good. It makes you feel good that you know what's best for someone else!

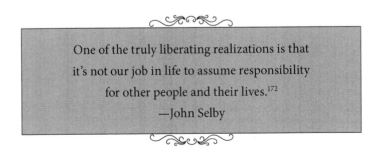

One of the truly liberating realizations is that
it's not our job in life to assume responsibility
for other people and their lives.[172]
—John Selby

It's similar to giving advice when no one has asked for it. People love to give advice. Again, there is a certain power that comes along with giving advice. "I know more about the situation than you do and this is what I would do. This is how I would handle it. This is what you *should* do." I love that one—*this is what you should do*. As François de la Rochefoucauld wrote, "Nothing is given so profusely as advice."[173] People give advice on what career path to take, what type of job would be "best for you," what foods to eat and not to eat, what to do with our money, how to raise our children... the list is endless.

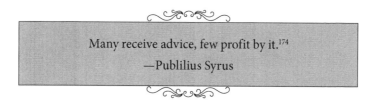

Many receive advice, few profit by it.[174]
—Publilius Syrus

Think twice before you offer unsolicited advice, opinions, or the dreaded *"It's for your own good."*

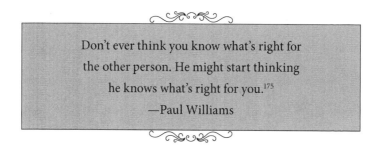

Don't ever think you know what's right for
the other person. He might start thinking
he knows what's right for you.[175]
—Paul Williams

SOMETIMES, YOU JUST DON'T KNOW

We don't know a millionth of one percent about anything.[176]
—Thomas Edison

Don't be afraid to admit that you don't know. Most of the time, we really *don't* know, but we would never admit it. It's refreshing to hear someone say that he or she doesn't know. So why do we feel that we have to act like we do know everything about everything? Is it that important to impress people with your supposed knowledge?

We're all familiar with the line, "Everyone hates a know-it-all." If this is true, why are we so quick to jump in with an answer? If everyone hates a know-it-all, why would we want to be hated? I believe most of us know that our ego gets in the way. We want to show how smart we are, regardless of whether we know anything about what we are talking about. We rush in with our answer before anyone else can.

It is readily observable that followers of religions are characterized by the presumption of "I know" via scriptural authority, ecclesiastical doctrine, historical precedent, and so on. In contrast, the spiritual devotee for nonduality starts from the basic, more truthful position that "I, of myself, *don't know.*"[177]
—David R. Hawkins

Why are we so afraid to admit this simple fact: "I don't know." Again, obviously the ego is at work, but just try it sometime when you are with your friends, coworkers, family, or whoever. They will be refreshingly surprised and will probably like you more, and believe me—someone else will jump in with an answer. As Ralph Waldo Emerson wrote, "When I cannot brag about knowing something, I brag about not knowing it."[178]

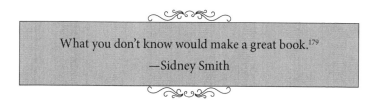

What you don't know would make a great book.[179]
—Sidney Smith

GO BEYOND

Boundary lines, of any type, are never found in the real world itself, but only in the imagination of mapmakers.[180]
—Ken Wilber

Most of us live in our safe little world, our comfort zone, our mapped-out world. We create this little world full of boundaries because it makes us feel safe. It is the known. We like the known. We like the known because it is the past. There is safety and security in the known. This is about going beyond the known—beyond living in our mapped-out world, beyond what we may believe to be true, beyond the cage we may be living in now.

It is good to love the unknown.[181]
—Charles Lamb

The problem is, we get used to living in our cage and we may even like it. Like prisoners who don't know what to do when they get out of prison, many have become so accustomed to being behind bars that it's difficult to live another way. As Arthur Schopenhauer states, "Every man takes the limits of his own field of vision for the limits of the world."[182]

There are few surprises when we live in the world of the known—and also not a whole lot of excitement. There also is little creativity. How exciting would the world and your life be if everything were known? You'd know what's going to happen tomorrow, next week, next year… and you would be bored out of your mind. It would drive you crazy. And yet, most of us live a life that is much like the one I am describing. We want the comfort and security, and we think we want the known.

I also like my known. I tend to have the same breakfast, read the same newspaper at around the same time each morning, drink my coffee while reading the paper, do my Sudoku, and then read the same types of books each morning, and eventually drive the same route to my business, except for when I make myself take a different route because I know I am living in the known!

It's easy to live in this safe little world, because I am used to it and there are no real surprises. I have to tell myself, *force* myself to do something different, to go beyond my normal way of doing things. Not that there is anything wrong with my "usual routine," but if I did the exact same thing every day, there would be no real growth, no creativity, no self-expansion. I would become the "usual me."

The world or reality has it limits, the world
of imagination is boundless.[183]
—Jean-Jacques Rousseau

Beyond is an interesting word. Beyond our neighbor's house. Beyond the horizon. Beyond our normal way of thinking. Out there beyond. Beyond lie the riches that we're looking for. In this case, beyond our habitual way of thinking, acting, believing, and living. Beyond what is known. Beyond the "usual you." Beyond all the concepts that you hold to be true.

That's what you're really looking for. You don't want the known even though you may think you do. Again, the known is the past. Let yourself enter into the world of the unknown, where all of life's treasures exist. Beyond the rainbow lies the pot of gold. That's where the treasure is. It's not at the start of the rainbow where you can see it.

A good traveler has no fixed plans
and is not intent upon arriving.
A good artist lets his intuition
lead him wherever it wants.
A good scientist has freed himself of concepts,
and keeps his mind open to what is.[184]
—Stephen Mitchell

If you don't know what's going to happen, that's exciting. If you do know, that's not. It's mundane, boring, lifeless. Claude Bernard said, "Man can learn nothing except by going from the known to the unknown."[185] The unknown is where scientists live and work. That's where discovery exists. They may try to disprove what is known, but most spend their time in the unknown. That's where creation is.

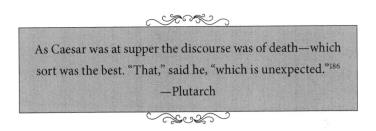

As Caesar was at supper the discourse was of death—which sort was the best. "That," said he, "which is unexpected."[186]
—Plutarch

Going beyond is not easy. It leads to the unknown, and you give up your safety and security that you think you have in the known. But you have to go beyond this way of thinking to ever realize your true potential, your true greatness. As Anam Thubten advises in his book *No Self, No Problem*:

> Go beyond everything. That means continuously embracing this understanding in your experiences, living it, feeling it in your gut, and integrating it with the totality of your life. The good and the bad, the successes and failures, are all part of the same duality—they are all like stories in a dream world, that only appears in the mind of the dreamer.
>
> During this stage we learn to maintain an enlightened mind in the face of all conditions. We maintain an inner wisdom that transcends all conditions. Through

embracing and living this truth, we realize inner freedom
that is the only nirvana to be found.[187]

Do as Thubten suggests and go beyond all the perceived dualities
that exist in life. Transcend all conditions. Everything in life is a
perceived duality, so why not learn to go beyond each and every one?
Don't get caught up in the highs and lows of life. Go beyond the good
and the bad, the praise and the criticism, the joy and the sadness, being
on top of the world one moment and down in the dumps the next.

David Hawkins writes in his book *The Eye of the I* that "To
go beyond the known requires courage, faith, and conviction. It
also requires spiritual power and energy whose source is innate
with the higher field of consciousness and the great teachers and
their teachings."[188]

Krishnamurti, the great Indian sage, wrote an entire book on
Freedom from the Known. Most of us would look at the title and
think, *Freedom from the known? Why would we want that? What's
that all about?* It was such an important concept for Krishnamurti
that he devoted an entire book to it and also most of his life. He
knew that we all live in this world of the known and that there is
a way to escape from it. He didn't necessarily use the words "go
beyond," but that was the essence of his message. He wrote,

> For centuries we have been spoon-fed by our
> teachers, by our authorities, by our books, our saints. We
> say, "Tell me all about it—what lies beyond the hills and
> the mountains and the earth?" and we are satisfied with
> their descriptions, which means that we live on words
> and our life is shallow and empty. We are second-hand
> people. We have lived on what we have been told, either
> guided by our inclinations, our tendencies, or compelled
> to accept by circumstances and environment. We are

the result of all kinds of influences and there is nothing new in us, nothing that we have discovered for ourselves; nothing original, pristine, clear.[189]

Are you a second-hand person? We all are to some extent and some of us to the fullest extent. But there is no originality in this kind of life. Nothing new. It's all known. Freedom from the known is what you want. That's what you need, and that is where uniqueness and creativity exist. Go beyond all your old beliefs, your usual way of living and thinking, and experience a new way of looking at and living life.

Don't be a second-hand, spoon-fed citizen. Do something different today. Go beyond your normal routine. Take a different route to work—you might be surprised by what you see. If you usually do thirty push-ups in the morning, do thirty-five. If you normally walk for twenty minutes in the morning or evening, go beyond that and walk for thirty minutes. Take a different path than you normally take. Instead of watching TV for three or four hours at night, read or write for an hour. That will still leave a couple hours for TV. Spend fifteen minutes each night learning a new language. Find out if there is something special in yourself that you didn't know existed. Go beyond the usual you.

My personal experience is that without transcendence, life has no beauty. In order to live a full life it is necessary to go beyond all boundaries. As the Sufi poet Rumi has said, "Out beyond ideas of right-doing and wrong-doing there is a field. I'll meet you there."[190]
—Deepak Chopra

YOUR GREATEST GIFT:
YOUR UNIQUE FLAWS

Owning one's own inner flaws allows for nonjudgemental respect for others and opens the door for compassion for all of humanity.[191]
—David R. Hawkins

Your flaws—or I should say, your perceived flaws—are unique because they are what make you "you." The majority of the imperfections that we see in ourselves are actually our personal mental fabrication of an imperfection that we think exists. This mental fabrication could be something that you conjured up in your mind today or in the past week, or it could be something that you have held onto for a lifetime.

We may have been told by others that we have this "flaw," but most likely we have told ourselves that we have this imperfection or imperfections. Over time, we start to believe it. We tend to be our own worst enemy! Once you start believing what you are telling yourself, it becomes your reality. But guess what? It's not true. It's only true because you believe it's true and have given life to it. You have watered and nurtured this flaw just like a plant. You have helped it grow and flourish. And the more you focus on it, the more it will grow. Because you believe it's true, you make it part of your daily life. *This darned flaw that I have to live with!* And so you go through your life believing that you and the flaw are one. That you *are* the flaw.

So now that you have bought into this perceived imperfection, believe it's true, and consequently have to live with it until you change your beliefs, there is a gift that comes with it. You are probably thinking, *A gift—are you crazy? How could this thing that has tormented my life be a gift?* Because out of this mental torment, this perceived imperfection, a true quality of greatness can arise.

This flaw that you think you have to deal with and live with can lead you to heights that you might never have reached if you thought you were perfect in every way. Your perceived imperfection can inspire you to become far greater than your inner flaw.

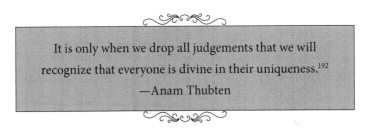

It is only when we drop all judgements that we will recognize that everyone is divine in their uniqueness.[192]
—Anam Thubten

If we were all perfect in every way, more than likely, we would tend to be less compassionate. We might also be lazy and not motivated to do anything great. If you are perfect, it would be difficult to relate to what other people are going through. Our inner flaws make us kinder, gentler, more compassionate human beings. They also inspire us to do greater things with our lives. We want to overcome this perceived handicap and achieve something better. To become greater than ourselves and our imperfections. To rise above them.

But perceived imperfections can also have the opposite effect. You may not be able to get past the so-called flaw. Of course, it's not really a flaw—it's only a flaw because you have given life to it as a flaw. And if you give too much life to it, you can become obsessed with it, leading to all kinds of frustration, misery, isolation, and ultimately depression. The more you resist it, the more it persists. The whole point of this chapter is to use your perceived flaw to your advantage. But for a moment, forget the flaw. Reverse your thinking about it.

I will give you an example. Let's say your perceived flaw is that you think you are too short. Obviously, in no way is that a flaw, unless you believe it is. Maybe you were teased when you were growing up, and it has bothered you for most of your life. As you continue to focus on being short, you start noticing everyone who is taller than you. You look around, and it seems that everyone is taller. The more you look, the worse it gets. It becomes magnified. Everywhere you go, there is always someone taller. The more attention you give it, the more it grows in your consciousness. You become obsessed. As you continue to make this scenario part of your life, it becomes the central part of your life—the main focus of your life.

And as you let this obsession become part of your daily life, it will become who you are. You will become the flaw instead of the perfection that exists in you. You have let this perceived flaw run and control your life. You are no longer in control. That is why it is so important to forget the flaw. Rise above it. In this case, reverse the thinking. Believe you are taller—not that you need to be. Start noticing all the people who are shorter than you. Better still, don't give it any attention at all. As you take your attention away from something, it goes away. It is no longer who you are. It no longer defines you. You can now define yourself.

I use height as an example because it is something we can all relate to. But I could have used hundreds of examples: nose too big, ears too big, complexion too bad, hair too straight or too curly… Or maybe you think you are ugly, strange-looking, too fat, too thin. "Too" is a word that you should stay away from, unless you use it to your advantage—too smart, too good-looking, too wealthy, too loving, too nice, too compassionate. How does that make you feel compared to those other "toos"?

Look around—there are an infinite number of shapes, sizes, faces. Which one is perfect? There isn't one perfect size or height. That's an illusion. The world would be a pretty boring place if we were all the same height, weight, hair color, personality, smile. Perfection exists everywhere if you see it. That is the key: you have to see it in your mind.

Many people have used their unique flaws to good advantage, making imperfections into perfections. We want to prove to ourselves that we are not this flaw that we have bought into. Many people go on to achieve things in their lives that they would have never achieved if they didn't have their unique flaw. There are countless stories of people overcoming hardships and handicaps of all kinds, transforming their lives, and achieving what seemed impossible.

When imperfection exists in the body (the life) of an oyster, sediment that just can't be removed, the oyster bathes it with layers of soothing coating, crafting it into a pearl. The oyster transforms potentially worthless, damaging, and unchangeable imperfections into treasures of value and beauty...

We all have misfit aspects of our lives, the "strangers within," waiting to be cultivated into pearls of wisdom. We can make this transformation once we accept ourselves unconditionally... doing everything we can to improve ourselves based on the conviction that our unique flaws are the raw materials of our unique treasures and strengths.[193]

—Taro Gold

Embrace your flaw. Make it your raw material for your unique treasure and strength, and you will achieve levels of greatness that you would have never achieved if you were so-called perfect. Love and embrace the flaw, because it is your greatest gift. And guess what? Once you love and embrace it, it will probably vanish.

12

Do You Really Want to Be Healthy?

Nearly all men die of their remedies, and not of their illnesses.[194]
—Jean Baptiste Moliere

I know this seems like a strange title. Who doesn't want to be healthy? We spend billions and billions of dollars on health care every single year. For a family with two or three children, the cost for health care is approaching or surpassing the cost of a monthly mortgage payment. Not only do we spend billions on health care and doctors, but we also spend billions on trying to stay healthy—gym memberships, jogging gear, personal trainers, diets, supplements, healthy foods, and the infinite number of books and videos on the subject of health. The pursuit of health and well-being ranks at the top of most people's priorities. If you're not healthy and not feeling good, all the money in the world suddenly is not that important.

So what do I mean by "healthy"? There are countless horrible diseases that plague society, causing all kinds of misery and suffering, and no one knows for sure what causes most of them. I am in no way making light of any of these diseases, and I know how much suffering sickness and disease can cause, not only for the person who has the disease but also for family members and loved ones. My focus in this chapter, however, is directed at some of the common, everyday types of illness like the common cold or flu. I have written this chapter to possibly change the way you think about sickness. Change the way you think about everyday illnesses, and it may change the way you think about other diseases as well.

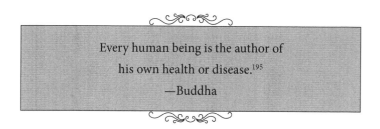

Every human being is the author of
his own health or disease.[195]
—Buddha

When I ask, "Do you really want to be healthy?" it seems like a silly question. You might say, "Why would I spend all this money on trying to maintain my health if I didn't want to be healthy?" The reason I ask this question, though, is because most people spend money on things outside themselves without ever thinking about what is going on inside their mind—their thoughts and beliefs about health and sickness. Most of us accept that sickness is a natural and unavoidable part of life.

Believe me, I used to buy into this too, until about ten years ago, when I started reading and studying some of the great authors and masters mentioned in this book. I used to think, *Great, a sore throat, and right before I go on vacation! Why does this always happen to me? Now the sore throat will lead to a fever and then sneezing, coughing, runny nose, and I will feel miserable for the entire week. Great! I knew this would happen!*

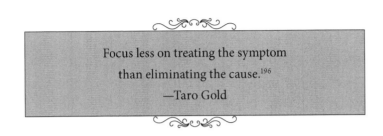

Focus less on treating the symptom
than eliminating the cause.[196]
—Taro Gold

How many times has this scenario played out for you? You accept it as part of life, because that is the way you grew up and you took it for granted that there is nothing you can do about it. I could always count on being sick at least a couple times a year. I hated being sick, but I didn't know that I had any control over what I thought was Mother Nature in action.

As children, despite how bad it is to be sick, there can also be some perks that go with it. You get to stay home from school, maybe watch cartoons or your favorite TV shows. You might be pampered by your mother and father, as in the old *Leave It to Beaver* TV episodes in which parents Ward and June always brought home ice cream to Wally and Beaver when the boys were sick. The bottom line is that despite feeling miserable, most of us received attention when we were sick as kids. As an adult, you don't receive as much attention, but a loving spouse may attempt to take care of you, you get to stay home from work, and you can still watch your favorite TV shows. Not a whole lot has changed, except maybe your choice of TV shows and the degree of pampering.

So besides the runny nose, fever, coughing, and feeling miserable, there may be some rewards for being sick, incentives not to be well. I am not implying that anyone wants to get sick for these reasons, but perhaps the desire to fight off sickness is diminished a little because of the way we are treated when we are sick. This isn't the case for everyone, but I think most of us have experienced some degree of pampering and attention when we have been sick.

This chapter is about changing the way you think about sickness and disease—exposing you to an entirely new way to approach sickness. You may think it's a bunch of nonsense and that we have no control over whether we get sick, and if you do think that way, what I'm suggesting most likely won't work for you. But how has your old way of thinking about sickness and disease been working out?

Do you line up like the rest of the masses to get your flu shot every year? I know many friends and family members who without fail get their annual flu shot—and without fail end up getting the flu. I'm not advocating that you should not get a flu shot; it may work for you, and if you believe it will work, that's half the battle. I mention flu shots because I have never had one. I also have not had the flu in at least ten years. I'm not telling you this to brag or imply that I have any special powers that you don't have—but I did change my thinking about sickness. I did a complete 180 in my thoughts on the subject. I personally found something much more powerful than a flu shot, at least for me.

The number of diseases is a disgrace to mankind.
—François de Salignac de la Mothe-Fénelon

I used to buy into colds and flus and believed they were an unfortunate part of life that you just had to deal with. Being sick was normal. No way around it. You accept it, you accept going to the doctor, and you accept being down and out for at least three to four days. That's the way life is. Fortunately, I had an awakening on how I viewed sickness and disease.

About ten years ago, I heard Dr. Wayne Dyer, the renowned author and speaker, discuss this very subject. He was talking about how he too used to buy into sickness, but after reading the messages from virtually every great master, prophet, and sage in history, he found that they all had the same message about health: it is not natural or normal to be sick. As Venice Bloodworth states, "It is natural for man to be healthy and whole in mind and body. When one learns this truth, and lives in accord with the laws of his being, health and prosperity spring forth naturally and abundantly."[197]

Dr. Dyer went on to say that he just told himself that, from that point on, he would not be sick. He was no longer going to accept sickness as a way of life. When he felt a sore throat coming on, he would go out for a walk or run and would not accept that he was going to be sick because he had a sore throat. He was not going to be sick again. He ingrained this in his consciousness as a new way of life. I have heard Dr. Dyer speak in person, and he said that after twenty years, he has had bouts with sickness and disease, but they have been rare.

Nothing is foolproof, as a variety of factors can weaken your immune system and your ability to fight off disease: lack of sleep, lack of exercise, stress, worry. None of us is invincible. But at least for me, the benefit of thinking in a new way far surpassed what I had been accustomed to. Getting a cold or the flu would now be a shock to me instead of the old, "Great, another cold!" Dr. Dyer's message inspired me. It motivated me. After hearing his message about sickness, that very same day I made up my mind that I would do exactly as Dr. Dyer did. I planted a seed: the health seed. The sickness seed was uprooted that day.

I was no longer going to allow sickness to be a part of my life. Sure, there was a possibility it might not work, but I was ready to give it a try. Why not? What would I have to lose by just changing my thinking? It wouldn't cost me anything. I made a vow to myself that sickness was no longer going to be just a fact of life that I would have to deal with. If I felt like I might have a sore throat or be coming down with something, I would do exactly as Dr. Dyer did. I would go for a walk or run. I would tell myself that it's not natural, that I was too healthy to be sick. That my immune system was too strong and could fight off any diseases, any germs.

And guess what? I stopped getting colds. I no longer got the flu. I went for about four or five years without being sick and was so confident that I would never be sick again that I made the dumbest bet I've ever made. I bet my brother $100 that I would never be sick again. The problem with the bet was that the only way I could collect would be if I died without being sick. Not very bright, but it motivated me even more.

Bruce Lipton points out in his book *Biology of Belief*[198] that our thoughts can affect every cell in our body. If that is the case, you can see how powerful this tool can be for us. So why not put it to work where it will truly benefit us? If you can affect every cell in your body, affect them in a good way. Use affirmations. Don't let the old thoughts of sickness and disease get a grip on the new you, the healthy you, the radiant you, the robust you.

> All disease is unnatural and does not belong to the *real* person—if it did, no one could heal it. Any doctor will tell you it is the nature of the body to heal itself of every disease, and that it is the nature of the mind to fight off every psychosis and neurosis. If they didn't, no one could be healed. There is no physician who thinks he heals anything or anyone. He only assists nature in re-establishing the normal process of circulation, assimilation, and elimination in both body and mind.[199]
>
> —Ernest Holmes

I had gone for about six years without having any kind of cold or flu, and then I came down with a cough and a cold. I was shocked, as I was starting to think I was invincible to sickness. Maybe it was a wake-up call, a sign that I was human. As disappointed as I was, I attributed the illness to a lack of sleep and my immune system being weakened. I can't recall what was happening at that point in my life—maybe I was stressed over something—but it affected my ability to fight off the sickness. I set myself up to be vulnerable.

The worst part (besides being sick after all the years of good health) was that I had to pay my brother $100. Still, I did not let this setback influence me. I knew that what I was doing was working. That is the only time I have been sick since I adopted this new way of thinking and believing. Being sick once in ten years—that's not bad, considering I used to get sick once or twice a year.

Every action has a resulting consequence (Newton's Third Law of Motion) is the commonly-held belief. For example, it is assumed that if someone has a cold, you can "catch it" through the transmission of germs. Does this always happen? Of course not. Why not? There are innumerable additional factors, like the state of the person's immune system, their nutritional constitution, their white blood cell count, and their emotional and mental health. If the person is in prime physical condition and manages stress effectively, they are less likely to "catch a cold" regardless of how much direct contact they have with the ill individual. The germs don't *cause* the cold—the condition for the cold to arise must first be present before the cold can manifest.[200]

—Scott Jeffrey

We want to be healthy. That's why we spend all this money at health clubs: to have better health and to feel good. But the point I am trying to make is, don't discount the power of the mind. Don't discount managing stress. Don't discount the fact that we can change the way we think about sickness and disease. It may be the greatest power we have in fighting disease.

I know what it feels like to be sick, and it's not fun. You feel miserable, and the last thing in the world you want to hear is some guy telling you that it's not normal to be sick. I don't talk to anyone about it now (except in the book and with my immediate family). There is no need, because most people wouldn't listen, and not only that, they don't want to hear it. It's not something you go around telling all your friends about.

But I can't stress enough how important it is for you to adopt this attitude that sickness is not natural. You are healthy, and sickness has no place in your life. You can start today and do exactly what I did and still do every day. You have the exact same power. You can start your journey of health now just as I did ten years ago. Jesus gave us the same message. He said that what he can do, you too can also do. You have the same powers Jesus had. You have the power to heal yourself, to be well.

The biggest stumbling block will be your faith and belief that it will work. If you are skeptical, think that I am delusional, think it's a hokey idea but that maybe you'll give it a try for a little while to see what happens, it may not work for you. You have to believe that it will work.

If you do happen to feel not quite up to par, maybe a bit of a scratchy throat, try this affirmation by John Randolph Price from his book *Nothing Is Too Good to Be True*: "I am the wholeness of the universe in individual expression, therefore, every cell, tissue, and organ of my body is in a state of divine order and perfect well-being."[201] Even if you feel good, it wouldn't hurt to read and express this affirmation in your daily life. It certainly won't hurt you, and it will hopefully inspire you. Say it now: that every cell, tissue, and organ in your body are perfect! How does that make you feel? If you repeat it enough, you might just start believing it. At the very least, your subconscious will. Why not give it a try?

> You must resurrect your mind from the consciousness
> of disease—from the thought of disease. You are
> the invulnerable Spirit: but the body now rules
> the mind. The mind must rule the body.
> —Paramahansa Yogananda[202]

You may still be skeptical and say, "I want scientific proof. Why should I believe you? My doctor has never mentioned this to me." Of course your doctor isn't going to mention it—that would be like me telling people not to eat candy. Doctors didn't spend all those years (and money) in medical school and internships to tell you that you don't have to be sick. Their livelihood depends on people being sick. You should actually pay your doctor every month that you don't have to go see them.

This is not an attack on doctors. Doctors provide an invaluable service to society, and I have the utmost respect for them and what they do. They are wonderful at making repairs, at fixing things that are broken, at giving medicine to make you feel better, at assisting Mother Nature. They deserve the money they are paid and are an intrinsic part of our society—when we need them. But they don't heal us. They don't have the power to heal. I am in no way telling you to stay away from your doctor and that you can mentally treat every disease. I use doctors whenever necessary, but I have made very few trips to the doctor because it hasn't been necessary.

> No intelligent physician of any school claims to do more than assist nature to restore the normal conditions of the body. That it is a mental energy that is assisted, no one denies; for science teaches us that the whole body is made up a confederation of intelligent entities, each of which performs its function with an intelligence exactly adapted to the performance of its special duties.
>
> It is a mental energy that actuates every fibre of the body. Health, like any other condition, is a matter of consciousness and is absolutely a matter of choice. Mind controls every function of the body. Take away your mind and your body is as lifeless and senseless as your front gate post.[203]
>
> —Dr. Thomas J. Hudson,
> as quoted in *Key to Yourself*

Let's get back to the idea of scientific proof. I did just what scientists do when they want to test a hypothesis: performed repeated experiments until I concluded that what I was testing was repeatable—that is, producing the same results. The main difference is, I didn't have a group to test. I could only test myself, and you might say that is where my scientific experiment is flawed. And maybe it is flawed, but I did put to test my experiment ten years ago, as I wanted to test the mental attitude that Dr. Wayne Dyer and countless others have proclaimed and practiced. I did my own scientific experiment on myself. I was sick at least two times a year before I put my personal experiment to a test. Since adopting this new state of mind about health, sickness, and disease, I have been sick once in ten years. So far, knock on wood, I have enjoyed good health—all because I changed my thinking.

The sage in this verse [Tao Te Ching] has looked long and hard at all illness, and has come to realize that it represents a physical manifestation of non-Tao thinking. A fever, a cold, an ache, or a pain are all identical to the non-Tao expressions of impatience, fear, anger, or any other ego-driven impulse. Since the sage has seen where thoughts like these lead, he refuses to participate in such folly. Thus, he has looked at poor health and vowed: *I will not think in ways that bring that about. I'll stay centered in the natural well-being of the Tao because to think a sick thought is to allow sickness to crop up.* Consequently, he's sick of sickness, and the result is the secret of perfect health.[204]

—Dr. Wayne Dyer

I too was sick of sickness and tried something different. I made a vow that sickness was no longer going to be a part of my life. That it was not normal, and there were going to be no more sick thoughts. And guess what? It has worked for me, and it can work for you as well.

Of all Western culture's beliefs, few reveal themselves as intellectually and spiritually bankrupt as those pertaining to health. For while medical technology has brought unprecedented sophistication to the practice of medicine, and scientific explorations daily uncover new secrets of the body's inner life, Western culture remains among the unhealthiest ever to people the globe. Billions upon billions are spent on health care; the rise of degenerative diseases mocks the technological advances which can never keep pace; and the cost of maintaining the health care system affects everyone, in sickness and in health.

You create your reality through your beliefs. Knowing this and observing the epidemic of illness permeating Western culture, what can you conclude about the belief systems underlying the culture's approach to the body and to health?

You are taught to believe that you can play no role in maintaining your health, that such must be left to professionals bestowing the benefit of technology to patch up the decaying heap you cart about beneath your neck.

Is it any wonder Western culture should be riddled with illness?[205]

—Ramón Stevens

As you walk down the aisles of supermarkets, it's mind-boggling the number of drugs that are available for every kind of disease and illness. At the first sign or symptom of any kind of illness, we run to the drugstore or doctor to get our medications.

We have gotten to the point where we no longer allow the body and its magnificent immune system to do its job. We rely on drugs to do that for us.

Now, there is a definite place and need for drugs. I just recently had hip-resurfacing performed in New York City, and if I'd had to do it without drugs… well, let's just say I probably would have been in a tremendous amount of pain. The pain would have been unbearable, and I am very grateful for the drugs I received. Thank God for drugs!

But we need to think twice about buying drugs for every little ailment that comes along. Dr. John Efferiedes, chief of cardiac surgery at the Yale School of Medicine, states, "I am anti-drug in general and I always ask and have patients ask exactly why a doctor is prescribing medication. If there is not a very strong reason, the drug should not be taken."[206]

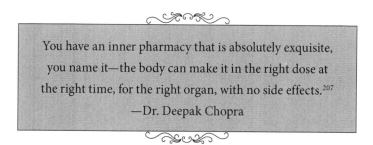

You have an inner pharmacy that is absolutely exquisite, you name it—the body can make it in the right dose at the right time, for the right organ, with no side effects.[207]
—Dr. Deepak Chopra

Doesn't it make sense that if we use drugs to fight off every ailment that comes our way that our immune system will no longer function as it was intended? It's similar to taking sleeping pills every night to help you go to sleep—pretty soon, you can't go to sleep without the pills. Without the drugs, you can no longer fight off illness.

Whenever I observe the rows and rows of drugs when I am in the supermarket, I always think about how humorous it would be to see animals in nature going to the drugstore for every ailment they have. Picture deer lined up at the checkout counter with their cart full of drugs. Obviously this is a ridiculous and crazy thought, but animals rely on what nature has given them—a fabulous immune system. Maybe that's why we are such a sick nation. Our bodies have forgotten how to fight off diseases.

The Swedish physician Carl Linnaeus wrote, "To live by medicine is to live horribly."[208] He made this observation back in the 1700s! Very astute. You can just imagine what he would think about the plethora of drugs and medicine available today. Again, drugs can be very useful and necessary, but don't dismiss the power of your body and its wonderful immune system.

Let's get back to the question of this chapter: do you really want to be healthy? Even if you don't believe or buy into anything I have said or what the sages throughout the ages have said— would it hurt to give it a try? There is no financial outlay. The only thing you have to do is believe that sickness and disease are not natural, not normal. Read the books by some of the authors I've mentioned. Learn for yourself. Don't believe it just because it worked for me or I told you. Do your own scientific experiment. Choose health and well-being. Where have your old thoughts and beliefs taken you except to the doctor's office and the drugstore?

The best advice I can give you if you want to adopt a new attitude about health and sickness is to change your thinking now. Do what I did—don't accept it. Believe that you are too healthy to get sick, that your immune system is too strong. Fight off the first signs of a sore throat and don't think that just because you have a sore throat that you will now get sick. Reverse your thinking.

Maybe it won't work for you, and maybe it won't work 100 percent of the time, but it won't cost you anything to try!

One of the hardest lessons we have to learn is that
we build our bodies by our thoughts; that they are
discordant or harmonious, diseased, or healthy,
in accordance with our habitual thoughts.[209]
—Orison Swett Marden

13

The Mythical Enlightenment

Enlightenment is one's destiny, not a goal, wish, or hope.[210]
- David R. Hawkins

Seeking enlightenment seems like a lofty goal but for most of us we hold the picture in our mind of monks sitting with their legs crossed in a cave somewhere in the Far East. They appear to be in a state of nirvana or an enlightened state or at the very least, some kind of trance. But is that something we can do? I personally don't have any caves close by and I'm not too fond of the idea of climbing in one to sit for however long it might take. It might work for the monk, but for the majority of people in the western world, it's not only not practical but you might be considered some type of freak if you attempted this – not that you should care if you are seeking enlightenment.

Just because you can't sit in a cave doesn't mean you should abandon the journey, the quest for enlightenment. As I have found on my never-ending quest for freedom, every day that I read, study, and practice the ideas mentioned in this book as well as all the teachings from the great spiritual teachers throughout time, I am "becoming" a little more enlightened each and every day. I do know that as I read, study, and contemplate these teachings, it's the best part of my day. It *enlightens* my day. And as David Hawkins says below – it is my self-evident Reality.

> The term enlightenment is semantically correct. It is the recognition and realization that one's reality is the light of the Self – and that it stems from within as an awareness and profound, self-evident Reality.[211]
> - David R. Hawkins

I try to incorporate my quest for enlightenment into all aspects of my day, which is difficult when you are at work with all kinds of distractions, when you are driving, going to the grocery store, running errands, paying bills, dealing with life. Life seems to get in the way of enlightenment and yet that is when we need it the most. There is a Zen saying that is applicable to life getting in the way of enlightenment, "Before enlightenment chop wood carry water, after enlightenment chop wood carry water."[212] It may not make sense to you but the essence of the saying is that as you become more enlightened, you still have to carry out the seemingly routine and mundane tasks of life. That doesn't go away just because you are becoming more enlightened. However, these mundane tasks can become more meaningful. You become more present when doing them instead of wishing you were somewhere else doing anything but what you are doing. You become more aware. The tasks still have to get done but now they are getting done with an entirely different outlook.

That is why I practice every day. I know that as I go through my day I am much more calm than I used to be, much more understanding, nothing really upsets me, things arise and subside and I know that. I stay in the present moment better than I used to. I feel like no matter what happens throughout the day, nothing really bothers me. I have an aloof feeling but not to my detriment where I don't care. I still want to grow my business, be active in it, be creative. I am still active in my family's life. And even though certain things are important, nothing is too important. You come to understand this, that nothing is too important. This is my journey with enlightenment and it is very freeing. Most of us have our own unique version of what enlightenment is to us, which is great, but the key is to make it our daily journey.

All human beings are already mystics and innately attracted to enlightenment, whether they are aware of it or not. It is an extension of the qualities of learning and curiosity, which are innate to the mind.[213]
- David R. Hawkins

You may think that you don't need enlightenment. Enlightenment being something for the people in the caves, spiritual seekers,… but not something for you. You might say something like, *I am fine with my current state and I don't have time to seek something that I don't even know what it is I am seeking.* But there is something inside all of us that wants something more and I am not just talking about money or happiness, both of which are fleeting. We want something more of ourselves. To become. Enlightenment is freedom. Freedom from all the beliefs and thoughts that keep us from being free. Free from perceived dualities, free from suffering, free from all our old beliefs that have not served us well. Free from all the man-made concepts that we buy into that are not necessarily true but we believe them anyway. Enlightenment for me is all of this as well as personal expansion and growth as a person. It is seeing perfection at all times. Will I ever reach this enlightened state? I hope not.

God, keep me still unsatisfied.[214]
- Louis Untermeyer

Deep down, I don't want to become enlightened. I know it seems like a strange thing to say after everything that has been said, but it's the point of this chapter. I never want to actually achieve enlightenment because once I got "it," then what would I do? I wouldn't have to read any more books, listen to CD's, practice on a daily basis everything that I have learned. I could just sit back and revel in my new-found bliss with a big smile on my face. I could then go through life "knowing" that I was enlightened.

And I would be bored out of my mind. It was never about achieving enlightenment. That's just a word. It can mean so many different things to each and every one of us. I am not sure how you would ever know if you were finally enlightened? Our true nature is to be continually expanding, growing, and aspiring. That is enlightenment. It's all about the process. That's why the monks and sages continue to sit in their caves or wherever they sit and mediate. They don't stop after a day of sitting, a week, or a year. They know it's a process, not a destination. It's a journey. I am always concerned that I am going to run out of books on the subjects mentioned in this book. That I will have finally read all the books that I could possibly read on these concepts. But it will never happen. There will always be an infinite number of books and authors available on these topics. I am continually amazed how one book leads to another and another and another... and my process will never be over.

To pursue enlightenment serves God and fellow humans. Be alert and attuned to the innate beauty of all that exists. See the charm and quaintness of whatever the world would considerold, beat-up, and ugly.[215]
- David R. Hawkins

There are many books that talk about how everything is perfect now. That there is no need to seek. This moment is perfect as it is. All of which may be true, but there is an inherent quality in all of us that is the same as life and the universe which is forever expanding. We need that continual expansion. That growth. That's what gets us up in the morning. Otherwise, we are like a river that doesn't flow, stagnant water which is muddied with scum. A flowing stream is constantly fed by a higher source and the water is fresh and dynamic. We need to be like this stream of fresh, dynamic water continually renewing ourselves. Continually being fed from a higher source. Continually expanding. We need it. We need the process. The process is the real joy, the real enlightenment. Each day in your pursuit of the elusive enlightenment, there is something new to learn, to practice, to meditate on… and each day you do this you will be a little more enlightened. We're like the professional athlete always striving to improve, to get better. The painter, the musician, the writer, the actor, the archer, the businessman, the scientist,… all continually striving for something higher. If the athlete accepted everything as perfect now, eventually his or her game would be similar to the stagnant water and their athletic prowess would soon become stagnant and their fellow competitors would quickly pass them by. We need that constant inflow from a higher source.

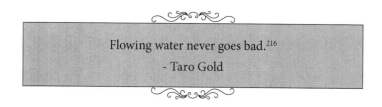

Flowing water never goes bad.[216]
- Taro Gold

As mentioned above, it's not just confined to enlightenment. It's true for everything we do. The end result can be great, but that's not where the real joy is. In business, I don't know what yearly sales figure I would ever be satisfied with. If your company sells one hundred thousand dollars in a year, the natural inclination would be to have sales greater than that the next year. If it's one hundred million, then maybe one hundred twenty million the next year (or more). Same for a billion. The amount doesn't matter. It's the growth – the process. That's what's fun. There is no end result. You may eventually sell your business, but it was the journey that provided the satisfaction and the growth in you as a person, not the dollar amount you get for your business when you sell it (although don't turn it down).

> The process of learning is often more
> important that what is being learned.[217]
> - Taro Gold

The same goes for almost every aspect of our lives. I am an avid tennis fan and I will use professional tennis as an analogy. It can also apply to the everyday hack like me. Each day the professional athlete practices, they get a little better. Each day they may learn something a little different, try something new, get in better shape, adjust their grip slightly, change their service motion. Each day is a process to make improvements from the previous day. Each day they are a little more *enlightened* with their game and may learn something they didn't know the day before.

And like most athletes, they have goals. Perhaps being ranked in the top 50 in the world, maybe top 10, or perhaps winning the US Open or Wimbledon. Once they reach these goals, they don't stop there – they want more. Sure they are happy and content for a while, but it won't last (unless they are retiring). They are all seeking something greater. Not because things aren't perfect right now, but because it is our inherent nature. Tiger Woods has won numerous tournaments including many majors and what does he do? Changes his swing and hires a new coach! You would think that would be the last thing he would do with the type of success he has experienced. But it's a continual, never ending process of improving yourself. It doesn't matter what endeavor you are pursuing. If you bake pies, you want to bake better pies. Same for horseshoes, equestrian riding, skiing, chess, dancing, piano, bowling, writing, business – it doesn't matter what it is, you want to improve. There is no final destination or resting place. Even in retirement there has to be a lingering feeling of, *Did I accomplish everything I wanted to accomplish in my life?* It's all about the journey.

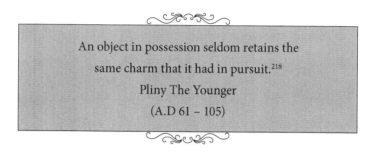

An object in possession seldom retains the
same charm that it had in pursuit.[218]
Pliny The Younger
(A.D 61 – 105)

As I mentioned, my favorite time of the day is the time I spend reading in the mornings before I start my day. If I were finally enlightened and no longer had to pursue anything greater, I know for certain I wouldn't be happy or content. I need the process. I need the growth. You need it. It's the growth, the aspiring, the expanding of ourselves – that's enlightenment. I personally never want to achieve enlightenment – but I want to come close!

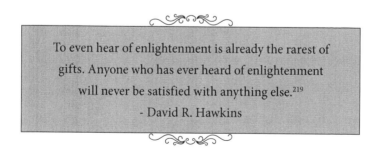

To even hear of enlightenment is already the rarest of
gifts. Anyone who has ever heard of enlightenment
will never be satisfied with anything else.[219]
- David R. Hawkins

Enjoy the journey.

14

Not Now!

This moment is eternity.

—Unknown

Every great master, guru, and sage throughout the ages has basically said the same thing: "This moment is eternity." They may not have used those exact words, but that is the message they conveyed. It is a simple message. This moment is all we have. Eternity exists in this moment. And yet many of us spend our entire lives either living in the past or in something we believe will be more exciting in the future. This moment is never good enough. There is always another moment lurking somewhere in an imaginary future that will be better. But not this moment. "Not now!"

> The power of the present moment is so immense
> it is capable—when lived in fully—of destroying
> forever every past mistake and regret.[220]
> —Vernon Howard

It's not an easy thing to do, living in the present moment. We tend to be continually thinking about something in the future that is going to be more exciting, more fun, more rewarding, better in some way or another than what this moment has to offer. Or we may be thinking about something that happened in the past, maybe a few hours ago, a week ago, or even years earlier, replaying over and over a situation that happened in the past. It's pretty rare when we are satisfied and content with the present moment. *It's just not good enough. This moment is not what I want. Please, not now!*

I try to remind myself throughout the day of this simple message: this moment is eternity. It's amazing how, if you will just say this to yourself a few times throughout your day, it will make seemingly routine or boring activities more meaningful. Standing in a line at the bank or post office, waiting in traffic, and other activities that used to seem like a huge waste of time will take on new meaning. You will start noticing things that you most likely would not have noticed before. Everything will be more vivid, not nearly as drab as when you wished you were someplace else. You are creating an entirely different outlook. As the Buddha said, "You have to make the present moment the most wonderful moment of your life."[221]

So what is meant by "this moment is eternity"? Most of us think of eternity as something that is in the future, not now. So we make eternity a thing, a place, a time—a place or time in the far distant future. But the present moment is all that can ever be. It's not future and it's not past. And that's all it will or can ever be. So eternity exists in this moment, *now*, not in an imaginary future.

> When your attention moves into the Now, there is an alertness. It is as if you were waking up from a dream… Such clarity, such simplicity. No room for problem-making. Just this moment as it is.[222]
> —Eckhart Tolle

I can't talk about the present moment, the Now, without mentioning Eckhart Tolle and including some excerpts and quotes from his books and teachings. Tolle is the modern-day guru of the Now, this moment. As I mentioned previously, he gave up a life in academia, gave up a career that would make any mother proud, to find meaning to his life. He was obviously not happy with his life (maybe felt he was drifting), gave up everything, and sat on a park bench… for two years! He literally sat on a park bench for two years. Talk about a long meditation session! And after two years, what did he come up with? The simple fact that this moment, the Now, is all we have.

He wrote a book about it—*The Power of Now*—and became famous. He has since written several books, has CDs, and does speaking tours, all from sitting on a park bench and coming to this wonderful realization. I love the fact that he risked a promising career to find what was missing in his life, to find freedom. His books are simple and elegant, and yet contain a powerful message.

> Whatever you do, act always in full presence of mind, be thoughtful in eating and drinking, in walking or standing, in sleeping or waking, while talking or being silent.[223]
> —Buddha

The Buddha also taught about the Now, the present moment. It's not just a modern-day revelation by Eckhart Tolle. Every great spiritual teacher has tried to convey this simple message. The problem is that as we get busy with our daily activities, our daily routines, it's far too easy to fall into the trap of living for a future moment or playing and replaying in our mind something that has happened in the past. It's so easy to do, and unfortunately, we can do it for the majority of our lives.

As we live in this fairy-tale future and relive the past, the present moment slips by. We are seldom aware of it and rarely live in it. As Taro Gold says in his book *Living Wabi Sabi*, "Appreciate this and every moment, no matter how imperfect, for this moment is your life. When you reject this moment, you reject your life."[224]

Living in the Now is not an easy thing to do, as we get caught up with everything we have to do in life. Life always seems to get in the way of some of these spiritual teachings! We all have things we are planning for, whether it's a vacation, a job interview, going to the supermarket, going to work, any event that takes place in a future moment. But if you recognize and are aware of being in the present moment as you plan for upcoming events and life happenings, you can appreciate much more what you are doing in *this moment*—because it's all you ever have. You hopefully won't wish you were somewhere else, anywhere but where you are now. But like I said, it's not easy.

I have a watch that for several years now has not worked. I wear it every day, but the time is always wrong and I have not fixed it. Why? Because it's a reminder for me that this moment is all I will ever have. A reminder to live in the present moment. A reminder to appreciate this moment now. Despite being late at times or not being able to give someone the time when they ask me, or even occasionally missing a flight, my watch is a great reminder to live in the present moment.

You don't have to go to the extreme of wearing a watch that doesn't work to live and enjoy the present moment, but maybe you have a ring or a bracelet or anything that can be a reminder for you every day to live in the Now. Living in the present moment is such a simple concept. But it's one that is very powerful and can make you enjoy life so much more. Don't reject this moment. Embrace it, and you will embrace life. Don't delay it to a future time – do it *now* and see how your life changes.

15

Our Highest Moment

The great thing is to try to fashion the life after the pattern
shown us in the moment of our highest inspiration;
to make our highest moment permanent.[225]
—Orison Swett Marden

We all have moments in our life in which we are so proud of
ourselves, so inspired, so elated with what we have done, that
it's almost as if we were having an out-of-body experience. Life
is magical, and we don't want the feeling to end. These are our
highest moments, our highest inspirations, but they are so hard
to hold on to! One minute you have it, the next minute it's gone.
Where did it go? Why does it have to leave us like that?

Most people forget their youthful experience of greatness and purpose or at least put it aside somewhere deep in their memory. It happens to all of us: We sub-optimize.

By sub-optimizing I mean that we may have an experience of the highest goal in our lives, but we quickly pull back to the lesser goals that society calls success. We often get frozen in our accomplishments, which may be great, but not the highest or optimal that we can attain. In other words, we settle; we sub-optimize.

In every moment we have a choice: will we act from the highest goal or recede to something less?[226]

—Michael Ray

I don't have a simple formula for making your highest moment permanent in your life; I am still in the process of making it permanent in mine. It's not always easy, as we can all become consumed by external activities and events. As you read and reread the wisdom from the masters in this book and practice what they are telling you, you may not succeed in making your highest moment permanent, but you will be a lot closer than you are now. I can tell you for a fact that the higher moments will be much more common. There will be far fewer down days in which your highest moments seem like a distant star.

> Man stands in strict connection with a higher fact
> never yet manifested. There is a power over and behind
> us, and we are the channels of its communications...
> This open channel to the highest life is the first and
> last reality, so subtle, so quiet, yet so tenacious... that
> although I have never heard the expression of it from
> any other, I know the whole truth is here for me.[227]
> —Ralph Waldo Emerson

You will still have the down days, but with your newfound wisdom, you will know they won't last. You will know that what arises does subside. You will no longer get caught up in the perceived dualities that used to take you for wild emotional rides. Even terms like *highest moments* are difficult to define because there is so much variation in them.

I think we all know what our personal highest moments have felt like, and we know that we want to hold on to them and make them permanent. Like I said, it would be impossible to make these highest moments permanent, but if you aspire to them every day, you are on your way to making them a reality.

I have listed some of my highest moments below. There are obvious omissions, like the birth of my children and getting married. Both are highest moments, but that goes without saying for most of us.

- I remember moments in business, like the time we chopped peanut-butter cups for twenty-one straight days to fill our first major order, as among my highest moments. The whole process—all twenty-one days, not just when we were finished. Sure, it was great to be done and a great feeling of accomplishment, but all twenty-one days were some of my highest moments.

- Running stairs at the stadium when I was in college at Arizona State is another high moment in my memory. I remember the weather being perfect and just feeling so good, so healthy, and so lucky. There was a feeling of exhilaration and euphoria, like I was on top of the world.
- There was the time I was running the trail at Mount Ogden Golf Course and the idea of chopping Reese's Peanut Butter Cups came to me. That was one of my highest moments.
- Seeing Notre Dame in Paris for the first time was a high moment. Although I am not Catholic, it was not only spiritual and inspirational but also awe-inspiring to me.
- Seeing the ocean live for the first time was one of my highest moments. So was chukar hunting on the Snake River in Oregon on a sunny day after it just snowed, standing on top of a ridge and peering down at the magnificent beauty of the Powder River running into the Snake River. Words alone can't possibly capture or do justice to the scene and the emotions I felt at the time.

There were plenty of other highest moments—in school, in sports, in writing this book, reading a great book, walking in Central Park in New York. We've all had moments like these, moments that you want to cherish and treasure and make them last forever.

But one of my fondest and most treasured "highest moments" was the day I spent with my daughter when she was eleven years old. Not that we hadn't spent a lot of time together, but this day was particularly memorable and special. My wife was out of town, and it was just the two of us. We did everything together—whatever she wanted to do. We made pancakes together, went to the mall, read, just hung out together all day.

What I remember most about that day was a book that I was reading to her about a small boy from India and how much he loved his father. The little boy's father was his whole world. His life and world revolved around his father. But this boy's father was dying, and I knew that while reading the story to my daughter I would get to the part where the boy's father passes away—and when I did, I could no longer continue reading. Tears welled up in my eyes, and I stopped reading. My daughter didn't ask me why. She knew. She knew why I couldn't go on. I didn't need to explain.

Yes, the story was sad, but it wasn't about the story or the book. It was about the two of us, together. Her love for me and my love for her. And that we wouldn't always be together like this. I knew that she would someday be grown with her own children, her own family, and that we might never experience a moment like this again. Those thoughts contributed to my tears. But they were happy tears—tears of joy for how much I loved her, for how much we loved each other. Tears of joy for that moment with her, just the two of us. I relished that day and still do, and I think about it often. I also think it's the highest of my highest moments.

I can't think of a grander aspiration than making your highest moments permanent. You may never succeed, but the journey will be worth it, I promise you.

16

Aspire for the Higher

Every normal-minded person believes in
something greater than himself.[228]
—Ernest Holmes

We all believe in something greater than ourselves. One way to achieve something greater is to aspire. "Aspire for the higher." It has a good ring to it. But what does it really mean? I can't give you an exact definition or a ten-step plan that will ensure your aspiring, but I can tell you that if you make aspiring a goal every day—not just once in a while, but every day—it doesn't matter whether you achieve something greater or higher, you will become a better version of yourself.

Aspire is a word that should not only be in our vocabulary but also incorporated into our daily lives. I dislike using words like *seeking* or *attaining*, because they imply something in the future, something that you can't have right now. But it is not always about the outcome. You may think otherwise, but you don't have to always have an outcome. Focusing too much on the outcome can take you away from the process.

> There is hope for the man who aspires: his place among the gods is assured. But he who hangs back and never dares and never takes action is withering on the tree of life, and all his wishes will not change anything as long as they are not strong enough to prompt him to attack his fear-created walls.[229]
>
> —U. S. Andersen

When you aspire for the higher on a daily basis, you are in the process of improving, growing, and expanding yourself each and every day. It doesn't have to be grandiose. It could be as simple as reading a new book, one that you wouldn't normally read, even if it's only for ten minutes a day. Perhaps it is a new routine of meditating for a few minutes in the morning or at night or both. Just try it for five minutes. It could be taking a walk for twenty minutes (if you typically don't take walks).

Maybe it's writing in a journal, taking some classes at your local community college or online, or taking tennis lessons, golf lessons, piano lessons. Maybe it's eating a slightly healthier diet—cutting out two of the four handfuls of potato chips you have at night before dinner, drinking water with your dinner instead of a Coke, or taking no seconds on dessert. Aspire for something a little bit better. It doesn't have to be grandiose. Grandiose can be too hard. Too much. Overwhelming. And then you do nothing at all.

> Attend only to daily growth, while never
> assuming you have reached full growth, and
> your advancement will have no limit.[230]
> —Vernon Howard

Initially, "Greatness" was going to be the title of this chapter. Most of us think of greatness as something that could be possibly attained in the future, but certainly not now. Greatness in most people's mind is something that takes a lot of work, that only a fortunate few are ever lucky enough to experience, something too overwhelming to try to achieve. I chose "Aspire for the Higher" instead because it's something we can all do now, not sometime in the future. When we do aspire for something better every day, we realize greatness. We experience greatness every day that we aspire.

Too many people believe greatness is a final destination, and if you are lucky enough to achieve it, you can be done with being great. Like climbing to the top of a mountain peak, you've finally reached your destination. But greatness is not a destination, a final resting place. It's a process and it is something that you do on a daily basis. It's the little things that will make you great. The bottom line is that we all want some form of greatness. Who doesn't? Who wouldn't like to be famous, a star athlete, a successful businessperson, mathematician, professional skier... or whatever your personal definition of greatness. But even if you did become a star athlete, successful businessperson, ballet dancer, you would still be aspiring to get better, to improve, to become more. Your greatness, regardless of what you think your greatness is, will always be a journey and not a destination.

"We can do no great things," wrote the nineteenth-century French saint, Teresa, "only small things with great love."[231]
—Stephen Cope

So what is greatness? It's a word we are all familiar with. Greatness for some may be mediocrity for others. Greatness for one tennis player might be winning the local club championship, while for another it might be winning Wimbledon. In business, it could be sales over a million dollars per year for one person, while for another it could be sales over a billion dollars per year. Greatness for one author might be getting a book published, and for another author it might be publishing dozens of books with several best sellers. It might be getting your dream job as a teacher at a school that you have always dreamed of teaching at. Maybe it's becoming the principle of a high school or a grade school. Perhaps it's becoming an air-traffic controller. Or maybe it's opening your own dance studio, or coming up with a new invention.

Greatness varies greatly (sorry), but the bottom line is that most of us want it. We all tend to believe that somewhere buried deep within us we have it, and it's just waiting to express itself at any time.

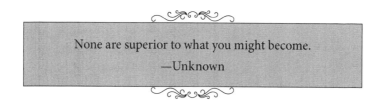

None are superior to what you might become.
—Unknown

As a child, you have visions of greatness. You talk to your friends and family about becoming an actor or actress, an astronaut, a business owner, a celebrity, a professional athlete, a doctor or nurse, even president of the United States. You imagine living in a mansion next to the ocean or owning a ranch with cattle and horses. Who hasn't heard or told these stories as a child? And then you become an adult, and what happened? Where do all those dreams and lofty aspirations go? How in the world did you settle into this comfortable job with good benefits and a good retirement? Where did the dreams go? Where did that child go?

Oh yeah—you now have responsibilities, and you're an adult, and no one from your family has ever been great, and you need the security, and only thirty-five more years until retirement, and then you'll be happy. Where did all that come from? Is it because that's what your parents did and their parents and their parents? Is it because that is what is *normal*? It's what society does? What happened to the dreams? What happened to your visions?

Obviously, if you are reading this book, then maybe this doesn't apply to you. You must want something different, unless you bought the book for the cover. But far too often, we give up on our dreams too soon.

What a tragedy to feel this is the best we can do with our lives. We are not confined to the habitual path.
—Vernon Howard

I will now tell you about a few things that happened to me when I was growing up that despite being somewhat silly do indirectly apply to aspiring and greatness. Hopefully there is a worthwhile message that you can take from them.

I don't remember much about my childhood, especially in any detail. I vaguely remember my grade-school teachers. I recall very little about what I was taught, but I do have vivid memories of a couple of things my teachers told me that were not overly inspiring.

I distinctly remember my fifth-grade music teacher making me mouth the words in the school musical. Mouth the words? Like my voice was going to ruin the rest of the fifth-grade choir? Embarrass the school? Up until that point, I had pictured myself as a decent singer. Obviously I must not have been good, but now I *knew* I wasn't good. It was the teacher's way of politely telling me that "you can't sing, and we don't want your voice ruining our musical." It wasn't devastating, but as a fifth-grader, it was memorable. Any time a teacher says something like that, it has an impact on you. And since those uninspiring words were uttered to me, let's just say I haven't been overly confident belting out a tune.

Also etched in my brain are the comments of my gym teacher in junior high telling me I was "physically retarded." We were starting tumbling, and I could not do a somersault very well, and then he laid that on me. Physically retarded? I was a decent athlete in school, but *physically retarded*? That comment along with "mouth the words" certainly didn't bolster my self-esteem. Being told that you can't sing and are physically retarded in grade school and junior high—those are things that stick with you! I remember very little about my education, but a negative comment from a teacher that you look up to and respect, that's something that can stay with you for a lifetime.

I am not telling you this to bore you with my grade-school inadequacies or somewhat benign experiences, but to show you how your visions of greatness can be eroded by society, by something that is said to you by a person in authority. It could be your parents, teachers, doctors, siblings, friends… and then you start believing them. You start believing that you are not destined for greatness because someone told you so.

What if they had told me I was stupid? That I would never amount to anything? That I would never be a success at anything? What if it was my parents telling me these things? Such comments can impact a person's entire life. That's why it is so important as a teacher or a parent to focus on what kids are good at, build them up, tell them that they have greatness in them. Instead of focusing on that one B, C, D, or F on your child's report card, focus on all the As or Bs. Tell children how smart they are and that with a little work they can get that C or D up to a better grade. Maybe math is not your child's strength, or he or she has no interest in math but excels in art and music. You can still encourage your child in math by providing help, but focus on areas of strength and interest, in this case art and music. Build your children up with what they are good at and interested in. Let them know that you believe in them and they are destined for greatness. Who knows—they just might believe you.

I will tell you a short story about an incident that happened when I was in college, one that I am not proud of, but it happened. It does apply to what is discussed here, and I will show how at the end of the story—so hang in there until the end.

I was attending Oregon State University, majoring in engineering, and I was taking my second term of calculus. A friend of mine and I went to see the professor of our calculus class to ask him questions about an upcoming exam. When we walked into his office, he was not there, but lo and behold, the test with the next day's date was lying on his desk, the very test that we would be taking! It was the apple in the Garden of Eden. And now the bad news—yes, unfortunately, we could not resist the temptation.

Looking down the hallways to make sure the professor was nowhere in sight, one of us stayed nearby his office on the lookout while the other went and made a copy of the test. It made for a few terrifying moments, as making a copy in those days wasn't just taking a picture of it with your iPhone. We had to find a copier, and we had to find one fast! Yes, it was out of character. I hadn't cheated in school before except for the occasional glance around the room while taking a test (and I am sure I am not alone on that).

But this was full-blown cheating. The Grand Poobah of cheating. The type of cheating that could get you expelled from the university. But we were young, we had tossed our morals to the wind, and we pulled it off. We spent three hours that night figuring out the answers on the test. That was probably two hours longer than I would have spent studying for it. Three hours for an exam that we were only going to have an hour to finish. The next day, as we sat down at our desks, the same exact test was placed in front of us. Not only was it a relief, but it was one of the sweetest sights in the world at the time. We looked at each other with a sheepish grin and began. Stay with me for just a little longer, as there is a redeeming quality (hard to believe) and a reason that I am telling you this.

We both finished the exam before the end of the class, while the rest of the class struggled to finish. We were the only two to walk out before the end of the hour. The next day, the professor said that the average grade was 45 percent. But he acknowledged that two students had excelled on the exam with scores of 95 percent and 96 percent. And guess who those two brilliant students happened to be? That's right, yours truly and my friend. The two cheats were beaming. The professor was amazed with how well we did on an extremely tough exam, and after class that day, he acknowledged our math prowess. He thought he had a couple of math wizards in his class. Little did he know that we were a couple of math cheats.

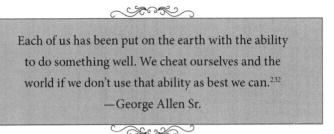

Each of us has been put on the earth with the ability to do something well. We cheat ourselves and the world if we don't use that ability as best we can.[232]
—George Allen Sr.

So you are probably asking yourself, okay, what is the moral to this story that has no morals? Well, it was the first test of the semester. Our professor now thought we were math whizzes, and we had more tests that we were going to have to take. We hadn't thought about that when we were busy pulling off the big cheat. We couldn't let the professor down. He would be more than a little suspicious if we both failed the next test miserably.

To make a long, sordid story short, I started believing that I *was* a math wizard. I started believing all the accolades he had heaped upon us. I had to work my tail off to become the person he thought I was and who I started believing I was. I studied hard, and I did well in the class. I started thinking I was great at math because my professor told me I was. I somehow put the cheating out of my mind and started believing my lies.

As it turned out, it was one of the best things that happened to me in my college career. Let me say that again: cheating turned out to be one of the best things for me in college! Obviously, I was extremely fortunate that there were no negative consequences from cheating. I could have been expelled from the university, and I would not recommend or condone it for anyone. But as you can see, there were good things that I took from it, and it did make me aspire for greater things, not only in math but in all my classes.

Am I proud of it? No. But it not only motivated me to become better, to become great, I applied that belief in myself to my other classes. You often hear of people who are liars who start believing their own lies. Well, I was living proof. I believed what the professor was telling me. I liked being told that I was smart, and consequently I excelled in that class. If I hadn't cheated, I would have done okay. Okay isn't great. Okay isn't something you write home about. Cheating made me start believing I was smart, and that is more than 90 percent of the battle.

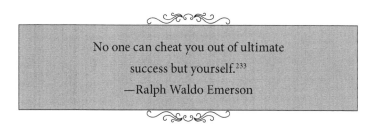

No one can cheat you out of ultimate
success but yourself.[233]
—Ralph Waldo Emerson

I tell you these tales from my youth to show how little things that happen during our lifetime can have a lasting effect on how we perceive ourselves. When someone in a position of authority believes in you, you start believing them. You start believing you are destined for greatness because someone you respect told you so.

You can see in these stories the vast difference of the prolonged effect of just a few words from people that I looked up to can have. I point out the cheating because even though I was delusional in believing my professor about being a math wizard, believing my lies, I did start believing. True or not, I bought into and believed it. And it was powerful. The same can be said for negative remarks—they too have a lasting and powerful impact on you and may be the reason you no longer aspire for something better and something greater.

I hope that after reading this book, you will acquire the wisdom and knowledge that you don't have to have someone else tell you if you are destined for greatness or not. You have it in you now. You don't need to hear it from anyone else. And the negative comments will also no longer impact you. Most importantly, you can tell yourself that you are great, that you do have genius in you. You now know it. You don't have to wait for your professor or your parents to tell you that you are great. *You* can do it every day. It can and should be part of your daily ritual.

You are the master of your greatness. You create your greatness—no one else does. And no one can take that away from you. No one can tell you otherwise unless you let them. You only cheat yourself if you don't realize that you are the creator of your greatness.

When the general habit of always aspiring, moving upwards and climbing to something higher and better is formed, the undesirable qualities and the vicious habits will fade away; they will die from lack of nourishment. Only things grow in our nature which are fed. The quickest way to kill them off is to cut off their nourishment.[234]
—Orison Swett Marden

Most of us want greatness, but the problem is, we want it now. We can't wait. We don't have time for the details. We want it now! We want our greatness now! We live in a society where everything is moving at a fast pace. There is no time for greatness. So instead of doing small things on a daily basis, aspiring to realize greatness every day, we do nothing. What it boils down to is that we don't really have time to be great.

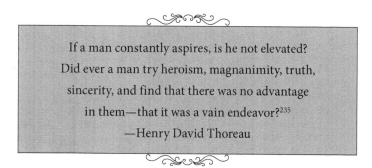

If a man constantly aspires, is he not elevated?
Did ever a man try heroism, magnanimity, truth,
sincerity, and find that there was no advantage
in them—that it was a vain endeavor?[235]
—Henry David Thoreau

The reason it has taken me so long to write this book is that I would often fall into this same trap. Sitting down the first day to write, chapter one, *are you kidding me? I'm starting on the first chapter, first page, first sentence, first word? Oh my God! I can't do this. It's too much. It will take me forever.* So I would put it off. *I'll start tomorrow. Tomorrow will be much better, I will be more inspired tomorrow.* And guess what? Tomorrow comes or this new now arrives, and I have the same thoughts, the same lack of ambition to get started. History repeats itself, and I do nothing.

But history does not have to repeat itself. You can change. The best way to change is to start. And a better way to start is to start small. We can all do small. Baby steps.

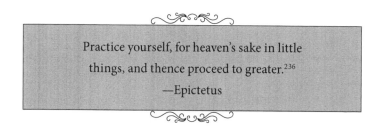

Practice yourself, for heaven's sake in little
things, and thence proceed to greater.[236]
—Epictetus

We, as humans, are no different from anything else in the universe (which is constantly expanding). We have this same innate need to expand, to grow, to become better. To not remain stagnant like a river that doesn't flow—and we've all seen what that looks like. We have to expand to feel good about ourselves, about life. That's why we aspire. It's in our genes, our DNA, our chemical makeup. You're either expanding or stagnating and contracting. That's why it bothers us so much when we are slothful and do the same things every day.

It's intuitive, and we know we have to grow and expand. It's the same for business. People wonder why Bill Gates, the late Steve Jobs, and other successful businesspeople continue to push for more sales, new ideas, new products. It's not about the money. It's about growing and expanding.

There is a divine hunger in every normal being for self-expansion, a yearning for growth or enlargement. Beware of stifling this craving of nature for self-unfoldment. Man was made for growth. It is the object, the explanation, of his being. To have an ambition to grow larger and broader every day, to push the horizon of ignorance a little further away, to become a little richer in knowledge, a little wiser, and more of a man—that is an ambition worth while.[237]
—Orison Swett Marden

Do the little things now. Do the little things in the best possible manner. Do the little things great. Start small. Aspire everyday. Aspiring applies to business, to life, to you. Focus on the little things and how you can do them well. Forget the outcome. If you aspire for the higher on a daily basis, you will achieve greatness on a daily basis. And I promise you—whether you do or do not achieve what you are trying to achieve with your aspiring, you will like yourself better, you will grow and expand as a person, and you will be greater, regardless of the outcome.

> We tend to become like our aspirations. If we constantly aspire and strive for something better and higher and nobler, we cannot help improving.[238]
> —Orison Swett Marden

17

The Ultimate Freedom

The only desire worth achieving is the desire for
freedom. All other desires are worthless.[239]

—Papaji

I have mentioned many times throughout this book that the resonating theme in my life has been a never-ending quest for freedom. This journey for freedom has influenced most of my decisions and career paths. My problem was that I didn't have a clue what I wanted to be free *from*. I was on this search, but I didn't know what it was that I was searching for, except that I intuitively knew I needed freedom—freedom from something.

What I have done, for better or worse, is chosen
freedom as my highest personal value and learned
to construct a life around that choice.[240]

—Chris Guillebeau

Unfortunately, until about fifteen years ago, I had little knowledge of any of the teachings mentioned in this book. I was as unaware as anyone could be. I went to church with my mother and two brothers growing up but knew very little of the teachings of Jesus, with the exception of his birth (Christmas was the best part of church) and his resurrection. One of the greatest sages/prophets/metaphysicians in the history of the world, and the only thing I remembered was Christmas, Easter, and that you needed to believe in Jesus as your savior and repent for your sins, otherwise the outlook for your afterlife wasn't rosy.

The only thing I knew about the Buddha was an image of some big fat guy in the lotus position, and metaphysics was as foreign to me as nuclear physics. I grew up in Eastern Oregon, with ranchers, cattle, cowboys, cowgirls, hunting, and fishing. Not much exposure there to spirituality, sages, or metaphysics.

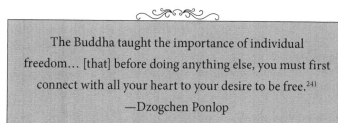

The Buddha taught the importance of individual freedom... [that] before doing anything else, you must first connect with all your heart to your desire to be free.[241]
—Dzogchen Ponlop

Consequently, I was unaware—and as Vernon Howard wrote, unaware that I was unaware. I didn't have a clue. But I knew I had to be free. I had this intense desire for freedom without the knowledge of any of these teachings. I think we all have this same burning desire for freedom, and it boils down to how much you want to pursue it. Are you going to make it your lifelong quest, or are you going to go with, "It is what it is"? Are you going to take the attitude that life deals the cards, and unfortunately, these are the cards I have been dealt?

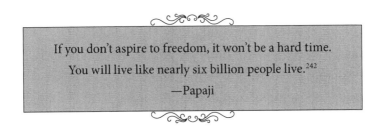

> If you don't aspire to freedom, it won't be a hard time.
> You will live like nearly six billion people live.[242]
> —Papaji

This never-ending search for me has always led to something better in my life. It has always taken me to another level of thinking and being, to new heights. As Robert Louis Stevenson wrote, "To be what we are, and to become what we are capable of becoming, is the only end of life."[243] I believe that a life designed around the pursuit of personal freedom allows us to become what we are capable of being.

After I graduated from college, I thought that a job, money, and possessions would make me free and happy. New cars, vacations, a new home, and then a bigger home, more money... and yet as I acquired some of these material possessions, I found that something was still missing. It always felt like there was some other freedom that I was looking for. I needed an escape from the world, from daily living, that would make me free. Not that I wanted to escape to a cave or live in a shack in the mountains by myself—not that kind of escape. But I knew I needed an escape of some kind.

How do you set yourself free from daily life? Wouldn't that basically be dying? In a way, that's just what I was looking for— not taking my life, but *dying to what I had been.* The death of the usual me, the death of all the things that I may have falsely believed to be true of life. Like cells in our body are continually dying to be replaced by new ones, I needed that type of dying of my thoughts, my beliefs. In *The Hidden Power of the Bible*, Ernest Holmes writes, "We wrestle not against outward things but against inward ideas and beliefs. The power of darkness is the power of false belief and superstition. If a man can change his inner concept his whole life will be changed. All cause is from within, all effect is forever without."[244]

I've always had this illusion that there is some large controlling body (society, media, bosses, parents, doctors, siblings, friends) that is continually trying to watch over and control your life. It is as if it were possible to group all these people and entities into one big controlling wizard, and then this wizard hovers over you and your consciousness at all times. This wizard is the gatekeeper of all your past thoughts and ideas on everything, and you need to conform to them—because the wizard is watching. Everything you learned from your parents, teachers, friends, family, grandparents, society, doctors, must not only be accepted as the truth but abided by. You need to conform to these truths, conform to the roles they want you to play.

This isn't about breaking the law. I am not talking about those kinds of rules and conformity. This is about truths and roles that we believe we need to adhere to because that's the way it has always been with our families, culture, society, and country for generation after generation. It's the generally accepted "rules and roles" of society. As Vernon Howard advises, "Don't live according to society's folly."[245]

But there is no wizard. There is no one central person behind or controlling society, the media, or you. It is all an illusion. All of these people are in their own little thought world and imprisoned by the same wizard.

> And we see in our society and all the societies around the world, that for every thousand people, nine hundred and ninety-nine are completely domesticated. The worst part is that most of us are not even aware that we are not free. There is something inside that whispers to us that we are not free, but we do not understand what it is, and why we are not free… The first step toward personal freedom is awareness. We need to be aware that we are not free in order to be free.[246]
>
> —Don Miguel Ruiz

The first step toward personal freedom *is awareness*. Since I was unaware of the teachings in this book, I was also unaware that I could free myself from this giant wizard and his rules and roles. I lived by society's folly. I didn't know there were options.

I didn't know that I could create my reality and make it any reality I wanted. I didn't know I could "watch" my thoughts come and go and not be affected by the negative ones in an adverse and damaging way. I didn't know that I could create good, constructive thoughts any time I wanted. I didn't know that I could think any thoughts I wanted and no one else had control over them—not even the wizard! I didn't know how powerful thoughts could be and that I was the captain of my own ship, the master of my thoughts. I didn't know I had thirty to sixty thousand thoughts a day—mostly the same as the day before, and the day before that.

I didn't know about awareness. I didn't know I had any control over disease and sickness. I didn't know I could be free of others' opinions, praise, and criticism. I didn't know that what arises subsides. I didn't know you were never born and you never die. I didn't know that we need to be continually growing, expanding, and aspiring. I didn't know that the Kingdom of God is within; I always thought it was a place in the sky. I didn't know of Jesus's teachings, the Buddha's, Lao Tzu's, and all the other great prophets, sages, and teachers, not only the ones mentioned in this book but countless others. I didn't know I could set myself free. Jesus said, "The truth will set you free" (John 8:32), but I didn't know any of this.

> But the moment that we pause long enough in the headlong rush of life to see that we are not moving in accord with or in response to our own decisions but rather in reaction to the world around us, then we have taken the first step toward freedom. Only one who knows his slavery can aspire to be free, just as true freedom is possible only to one who has experienced chains.[247]
>
> —U. S. Andersen

I was enslaved. Imprisoned. Not only was I unaware, and unaware that I was unaware, I was also clueless. I didn't know that I didn't know. Consequently I had imprisoned myself in this wonderful world and life that we are all engulfed in and it engulfed in us. I put the shackles on myself. I imprisoned myself. Is there any wonder why I have been on this freedom quest all these years? I didn't know there was another way to live. No one told me.

> In the end, it will be found that the sacrifice of letting go
> of the mind is actually the greatest gift one can receive.[248]
> —David R. Hawkins

This is the freedom I have been searching for all these years. It wasn't school, parents, teachers, money, security, that I wanted freedom from. I wanted all the freedoms mentioned in this book, and I am the master of all of them. It was never complicated. It was simple. I create my own destiny. I create my own freedom. I create my own reality. I am the creator of everything in my world. It doesn't come from anything external. It all comes from within. This is the heaven Jesus talked about: "The kingdom of God is within you" (Luke 17:21).

> No man can live a full life while he is bound in
> any part of his nature. He must have freedom of
> thought as well as freedom of action to grow to
> his full height. There must be no shackles on his
> conscience, no stifling of his best powers.[249]
> —Orison Swett Marden

And the freedom journey doesn't stop here. It will never end. The path to freedom stretches beyond anything I can imagine. But I will always be on it. This path has been *by far* the best thing in my life. You may say "What about your children, your spouse, your family? How could it be better than them?" And my answer would be that the freedoms mentioned have allowed me to love and appreciate my family far more than I ever could have before. I also finally know what I was searching for. I have found it, but it will always be a journey, a process that never ends. And in that lies its beauty.

I call that mind free, which resists the bondage of habit, which does not mechanically repeat itself and copy the past, which does not live on old virtue, which does not enslave itself to precise rules, but forgets what is behind, listens for new and higher monitions of conscience, and rejoices to pour in fresh and higher exertions.[250]
—William Ellery Channing

18

And Finally... I Don't Think So

A painting is never finished—it simply stops in interesting places.[251]
—Paul Gardner

This book is much like life in that the ideas, thoughts, message, and essence will continue on even after you turn the last page. The essence of the book, as in all books, music, art, and paintings, is eternal. It doesn't die. Your true essence and consciousness are much like the beauty of the painting, the music from your stereo, the essence of the book.

> To be alive is the biggest fear humans have. Death is not the biggest fear we have; our biggest fear is taking the risk to be alive—the risk to be alive and express what we really are.[252]
> —Don Miguel Ruiz

In my reading and studying, I have found that authors, sages, prophets, and gurus throughout the ages have delivered the same universal message: you were never born and you never die. You are not just your body. The essence and consciousness of who you are is timeless and eternal, with no beginning and no end. Let me repeat that: *you were never born and you never die.*

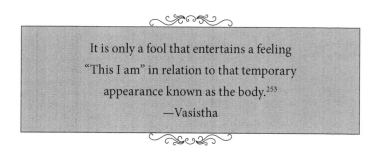

It is only a fool that entertains a feeling
"This I am" in relation to that temporary
appearance known as the body.[253]
—Vasistha

It's a difficult concept to grasp. If you have not been exposed to these teachings, you may resist or reject this concept, saying things like, "What do you mean I am not my body? That I wasn't born and don't die? I have spent a lifetime dealing with this thing I call my body, along with its mind and ego. Do you have any idea how much suffering it has caused me? The ten thousand pounds that I have shed and put back on, the countless visits to the gym, the running, the sit-ups, the push-ups, trainers, diets, the pimples and zits as a teenager, the days I felt like hell and yet still had to deal with all the aches, pains, and heartaches... No, you are not going to tell me that I am not my body. Can you begin to understand how much mental suffering I have gone through the past fifty, sixty, seventy, eighty years? The trips to therapy, the prescription drugs, the visits to the doctors, dentists, hospitals? I have way too much time and money invested in this body/ego/personality. How dare you say that I am not my body? I have spent a lifetime cultivating and polishing this person, this personality named [your name here]. Who would I be without all of this?"

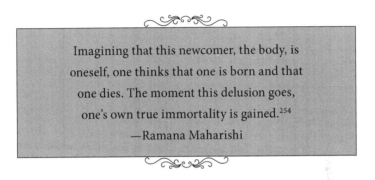

Imagining that this newcomer, the body, is oneself, one thinks that one is born and that one dies. The moment this delusion goes, one's own true immortality is gained.[254]

—Ramana Maharishi

I won't go into great detail on this concept, as it is beyond the scope of this book, but do think about this: *Are* you your body, your mind, your personality? Is that who you are? If so, which body, mind, personality do you choose? The one when you were four? When you were twenty? Fifty? Seventy? The body and mind I had at four, twenty, forty, I no longer recognize. I look at pictures from adolescence, teen years, early adulthood, and ten years ago, and that body and mind no longer exist. Virtually every cell in my body has died and been replaced. My essence lives on, but the body and mind of those times is nowhere to be found.

We fancy ourselves as concrete things, something with boundaries, unchanging, and when we have occasion to refer to ourselves or examine ourselves introspectively, we believe we know what we refer to and are adamant in our avowal of self. The truth is we neither know ourselves nor are we the same from one moment in our lives to the next. It is nearly impossible even for families to recognize a loved one after thirty years of absence, so greatly has the self altered.

And a little refection upon the changing quality of consciousness is sure to give us some insight into the numberless selves our surface minds and ego have become since first appearing in the world.

Shakespeare perceived the many masks donned by the Secret Self in its journey through life: *First the infant, mewling and puking, then the schoolboy with his shining morning face, then the lover, sighing like a furnace, then the soldier, full of strange oaths, then the justice, in fair round belly, then the lean and slippered pantaloons, then second childishness, then sans teeth, sans eyes, sans taste, sans everything.*[255]

—U. S. Andersen

Let's create a hypothetical scenario in which, as soon as you were born, you were taken away from your parents and had to exist on your own without any other human interaction for your entire life. Somehow you were kept alive. Even though it's ridiculous and could never happen, hear me out. You would not have parents, so you would not have a name. You would not have any interactions with other humans, so the concept of age, old age, sickness, and death would not enter your mind. You would be existing much like an animal in the wild, with your natural instincts for survival, but all the baggage that you have accumulated over time from society, friends, parents, teachers, and doctors would be nonexistent. The personality that you have now would not exist, as it is a collection of all your influences and interactions from the past. The "you" that you think you are would not be.

If I asked you right now to describe to me who you are but you could not use your name, job title, family, education, or anything that has happened to you in the past, what would you say? Try it right now. Write on a piece of paper or say aloud who you are without using your name or anything from the past. Who are you? Not as easy as you may think, but in actuality, it is easy. It is similar to the story in the Bible of Moses speaking to God in the burning bush when Moses asked God who he should tell the Israelites sent him. And God replied, "Tell them 'I Am' sent you" (Exodus 3:13-14). Like God, you too are "I Am." The only difference is that you may not know it.

So what is meant by "I Am?" Obviously no one knows for certain, but God didn't tell Moses to tell the Israelites that "God" sent him. He didn't use a name. And what is implied is that God is everything. Not a name. Not a person. Just "I Am." I Am the tree. I Am the sky. I Am the rock. I Am you. I Am that. I Am consciousness.

I AM is the self-definition of the absolute, the foundation on which everything rests.

I AM is the self-definition of God.

I AM hath sent me unto you.

I AM THAT I AM.

Be still and know that I AM God.

You are God. You are the "I AM that I AM." You are consciousness. You are the creator. This is the mystery, this is the great secret known by the seers, prophets, and mystics throughout the ages. This is the truth that you can never know intellectually.

Who is this you? That it is you, John Jones or Mary Smith, is absurd. It is your greater self, your deeper self, your infinite being. Call it what you will. The important thing is that it is within you, it is you, it is your world.[256]

—Neville Goddard

The person who lives in my make-believe scenario above would also describe himself or herself as "I Am." The person would exist as consciousness in a human body without ever realizing he or she is human. There would not be all the drama that we have created in our lives, our personalities, our past and future worries. This person would be living in the moment, trying to survive, but not dwelling on death because it would have no meaning. This whole concept of who we are, our personality, our ego, is everything we have accumulated in the past from interactions with other people. People have told us who we are, and most of us believe it!

> It's my experience that we're much more afraid that there might be a God than we are that there might not be.[257]
> —Julia Cameron

Have you ever had a moment when you suddenly stopped what you were doing and said, "Who am I?" Out of the blue, you look in the mirror and ask yourself, "Who am I?" You had this strange sensation for a fleeting moment that you were not this personality named [your name]. For a brief moment, you felt like you were no one. That there was no "[your name]." It's an odd feeling and rarely happens, but when it does, I think this is when you are experiencing your true self, who you really are. At that moment, you realize that you are everything, not just a body and personality. At that moment, you are existing as Consciousness; you are experiencing the infinite. At that moment, you understand there is no death, because who is there to die? You too are I Am, and you are on the road to freedom.

Ultimately each of us is a distinct consciousness in a human body, a unique part of a universal consciousness. We are like snowflakes of consciousness—each a little different but part of the Whole. That is our true identity. That is our true beauty.

When all the layers of false identity have been stripped off, there is no longer any version of that old self. What is left behind is pure consciousness. That is our original being. That is our true identity. Our true nature is indestructible. No matter whether we are sick or healthy, poor or wealthy, it always remains divine and perfect as it is. When we realize our true nature, our life is transformed in a way we could not have imagined before. We realize the very meaning of our life and it puts an end to all searching right there.[258]

—Anam Thubten

The body is much like this book with its cover, pages, and ink. It is the canvas of the painting or the paint. It is the components of the stereo, the CD. It is the hardware for the computer. All of these can be destroyed, damaged, burned to ashes, just like the human body. But it's not the physical components that make any of these things meaningful. You don't love the cover of the book or CD. You might like it, but it's not the reason you purchased it. You wouldn't buy a book with no writing or message, a CD with no music, or a blank canvas—unless of course you were going to paint or write. You buy them for the music, the art, the message, all of which are eternal.

One of your family members loses an arm or a leg, but you still love him or her the same. That hasn't changed. Your loved one could be lying in a coma with most of his or her body missing, and you would still have the same love you have always had for that person, if not more. The body parts might be gone, but it would have no effect on your love. It wasn't the arm or leg you were in love with. Your love is eternal for that family member regardless of what happens to the body or mind.

To unify with Life, to get in tune with the Infinite, is every man's search, whether or not he is conscious of the fact...

You could not think a thought if it were not for the intelligence of Life. You could not exist without It because It is you. Since this is so, you will never cease to exist—you will always be more and never less yourself.[259]

—Ernest Holmes

Most of us live entirely by our five senses. Our realty is our sense world—that which we can see, touch, smell, taste, and hear. There is nothing wrong with this; at times, it can be quite practical and useful. But it also limits us and imprisons us. We only see a very narrow part of the wide electromagnetic spectrum. We only hear at limited frequencies. And yet we base our entire world and life on this limited perception. We believe in our senses.

It is an established fact that our five senses perceive but the tiniest portion of the almost infinite spectrum of vibrations that prevails in the universe, that a million times more remains untold about each thing than can possibly be perceived by sensual means.

In short, the materialist who prides himself on accepting nothing but the evidence of the senses is accepting the sketchiest of evidence; he actually prides himself on his blindness, accepting things as facts on the basis of knowing a mere one billionth of their total qualities.

He would not dream of entering a business deal with such meager knowledge, but accepts the world and others and himself on such evidence and rears like a reluctant stallion when it is suggested to him that he lives among phantoms.[260]

—U. S. Andersen

I will give you one more make-believe scenario in which you have the capability to see not only the smallest particles that we are aware of (atoms, subatomic particles) but also countless others that we don't have names for yet or have not yet discovered. If you had this ability, when you looked at another human, a tree, a table, a car, everything would look the same. It might be similar to looking at the sky. That's why we are considered to be 99.99 percent space. With our newfound ability to see, our new perception, we would see only space. So where would this character we call "[your name]" start and end? Or the tree? Or the car? If you were looking at me, there would be no beginning to Tim. No boundaries to Tim. No ending to Tim.

> I can tell you as a result of my research about atoms this much: There is no matter as such. All matter originates and exists only by virtue of a force... We must assume behind this force the existence of a conscious and intelligent mind. This mind is the matrix of all matter.[261]
> —Max Planck, Nobel Prize winner for physics

We are part of one universal whole, one universal consciousness, one universal intelligence, one universal God, one universal whatever-you-want-to-call-it, one universal life. We are immersed in it.

We are not separate little entities existing in our own little worlds, although many people live their entire lives this way and thus the cause for all the suffering and the concept of birth and death. That's the suffering the Buddha was talking about. He wasn't talking about times being tough. Not physical suffering. It was mental suffering caused by this identification with a separate person, personality, ego.

The real you will always be. The real you was never born and will never die. You are immersed in this universal consciousness, universal intelligence, universal mind, universal perfection, God—and it is immersed in you. You just can't *see* it. Fortunately, there were and are enlightened beings who could and can see it, who could perceive this intelligence—great masters like Jesus, the Buddha, Lao Tzu, and many other saints, prophets, and sages throughout the ages. They have told us about it, and when we understand this truth, that is our awakening, our freedom, our immortality.

> You are immortal; not your body, not your Conscious Mind, but the real you, the part of you which exists forever in the Universal Subconscious Mind. You always have been: you always will be. You are inseparably one with everything that is, each human being in this world, all life, all form, all objects.[262]
> —U. S. Andersen

Have you ever felt like you have not been here? Have not been a part of life? I personally haven't. I feel that I have always been. You look at rocks, trees, the ocean, all of nature, and you have this feeling that you have always been a part of it. Everyone is consumed by what happens after we die, but no one talks about that awful time before our birth, that infinite period of time before we were supposedly born. If there were an infinite period of time before we were born, how could we be born? It would be impossible. Time would never reach our birthdate. That's why the sages and prophets have all said *this* moment is eternity. Eternity is not someplace in the sky, in the future. It is this moment.

> I believe in Life before Death.
> —Bumper Sticker

The kingdom of God is in us *now*, not at a time in the future. The kingdom of heaven is here *now* for all of us, not just for a chosen few who happen to be lucky enough to have been born into the right religion, or to have picked the right religion. It is available to all of us, this moment. Jesus, one of the greatest spiritual philosophers and metaphysicians the world has ever known, also said that we are immortal—that God "is not a God of the dead but the living" (Mark 12:27).

The universe is infinite and so are we. You are in the universe, and the universe is in you, continually expanding, growing, and renewing. That's what we do every day. Cells are dying every day, only to be replaced and renewed. Are the cells that are dying "you"? You are on a never-ending journey of renewal. Every day, you are renewing yourself—infinite renewal. That is the real you.

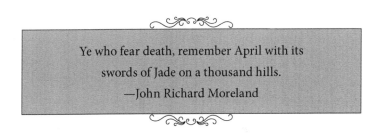

Ye who fear death, remember April with its
swords of Jade on a thousand hills.
—John Richard Moreland

As much as I believe in the teachings expressed here, I don't have an answer for the sadness, pain, and suffering caused when a close family member passes on or is physically no longer with us. The love I have for my family and my children could never be duplicated. I know that our physical bodies can't last forever, as the earth could not physically accommodate that many bodies. It would be impossible. The world, our life, our universe is perfect the way it is now. It could not be more perfect.

The poet Alfred Lord Tennyson affirmed that for him the feeling of being totally free of boundaries was "not a confused state but the clearest of the clear, the surest of the sure, utterly beyond words—where death was an almost laughable impossibility." This certainty was a tribute to the clarity of his experiences. In keeping with many others who have transcended the waking state, Tennyson concluded that those rare instances when individuality "seemed to dissolve and melt away into boundless being" had shown him "the only true self."[263]
—Deepak Chopra

You wouldn't want *this* physical body to last forever. That would be like a football game that never ends, a tennis match that goes on for infinity, a soccer game played for eternity. It would be hell, because it would be so boring. And if it were possible for your body to be around for eternity, which physical body/mind would you choose? The child, the teenager, the thirty-year-old, the fifty-year-old? For me, I want my children younger, my parents older, and my grandparents older than my parents. I don't want to be the same age as all of my family for eternity.

The universe, God, intelligence, life could never be designed more perfectly. The greatest scientists in the history of the world could never come up with anything remotely as magnificent. An acorn into an oak tree? There is not a scientist in the world who could conjure up something like that in a lab. What is the cause behind all of this? Where does this intelligence come from? That's the great mystery.

Despite the perfection and intelligence, what can make up for the loss of a loved one not physically being with us now? The physical loss of a child? And will we be together again? I don't know, but if we trust in the universe and its perfection as we know it, trust in its universal intelligence, we should never have to worry. For myself, an artist, engineer, designer, painter, beautician, or scientist could not in a billion years come up with a more perfect design for my children. If I personally tried to design or create the perfect children for me, I could not have come close to what I have been blessed with. Not in my wildest imagination. How could I be so lucky? How could I be randomly chosen to have the perfect children for me and my wife? For my life, for my personality, for me, they were and are perfect.

But it wasn't *just* me. I wasn't handpicked. I'm not the chosen one. We all are. It's true for all of us. That's the magic, the perfection, the universal intelligence, life, God at work. The acorn to an oak tree. How could it be more perfect?

We have to trust this perfection, believe in this perfection of the universe, the source, God, life. It's simple and beautiful and could never be duplicated in a better way. Know this and you will never worry about "death" again. That is immortal life.

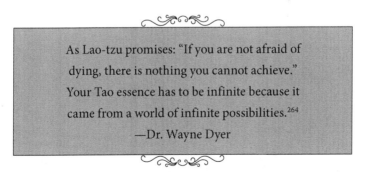

As Lao-tzu promises: "If you are not afraid of dying, there is nothing you cannot achieve." Your Tao essence has to be infinite because it came from a world of infinite possibilities.[264]
—Dr. Wayne Dyer

Even though I believe in these teachings with great passion, I tell you that you need to find out for yourself. You need to read the authors quoted in this book, and there are countless other books and writings that you can find on these topics. It has nothing to do with your religious beliefs, and I am in no way trying to persuade you to change the beliefs you may have. Any religious or spiritual beliefs should be enhanced by what is discussed in this book, not diminished.

But I will tell you that I believe passionately in the messages conveyed in this book. And even though I can't prove anything as being true, it is true for me. As Jesus said, "The truth will set you free" (John 8:32). It has set me free. You will need to find out for yourself if it is true for you.

When you return to your Self, this is called awakening, liberation, freedom. Having known your Self, you know everything. In this awakening the whole universe is discovered to be within yourself. All universes are within you, and you are the universe. This is ultimate understanding. Knowing this, you know everything. If you don't know this, you know nothing, regardless of how much information you collect. Without this knowledge, you are ignorant. Having known the absolute, you are everything—without beginning, middle, end, without birth or death. Here, all fears end.[265]

—Papaji

There is no beginning and no end. And I too will be back again and again and again and again and again. Maybe next time with, *Are You Still Drifting?*

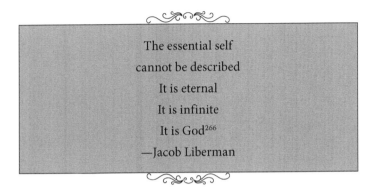

The essential self
cannot be described
It is eternal
It is infinite
It is God[266]
—Jacob Liberman

Recommended Reading

Below is a collection of some of my favorite books and authors. Most of the authors have numerous books that are available, and I would highly recommend any of the books from these authors. I have listed my personal favorites from each author. The books and authors are listed in no particular order.

Title	Author
No Self, No Problem	Anam Thubten
The Magic in Your Mind	U. S. Andersen
Ruling Your World	Sakyong Mipham
Inspiration	Dr. Wayne Dyer
World Enough and Time	Christian McEwen
Power, Freedom, and Grace	Deepak Chopra
Creative Ideas	Ernest Holmes
The Artist's Way	Julia Cameron
The Fifth Agreement	Don Miguel Ruiz and Don Jose Ruiz
The Power of Your Supermind	Vernon Howard
The Art of Non-Conformity	Chris Guillebeau
The Wonder of Being	Jeff Foster
He Can Who Thinks He Can	Orison Swett Marden

Nothing Is Too Good to Be True	John Randolph Price
The Power of Now	Eckhart Tolle
Transcending the Levels of Consciousness	David R. Hawkins
Journey to the Impossible	Scott Jeffrey
Conscious Life: Creating Your Reality	Ramón Stevens
Biology of Belief	Bruce Lipton
The "I Am" Discourses, Vol. 3	Saint Germain
Believe in Yourself	Dr. Joseph Murphy
Breaking the Habit of Being Yourself	Dr. Joe Dispenza
Key to Yourself	Venice Bloodworth
Living Wabi Sabi	Taro Gold
In Pursuit of Elegance	Matthew E. May
The Highest Goal	Michael L. Ray
It's Called Work for a Reason!	Larry Winget
The Science of Mind	Ernest Holmes
The 50 Year Dash	Bob Greene
Zen Mind, Beginner's Mind	Shunryu Suzuki
The Spontaneous Healing of Belief	Gregg Braden

Endnotes

Introduction

1. U. S. Andersen, *The Magic in Your Mind* (Important Books, 2012).

2. "Wisdom of Heraclitus," EmpHasise, http://enghweeong. wordpress.com/2009/01/07/wisdom-of-heraclitus/.

3. Andersen, *The Magic in Your Mind.*

4. "Lord Byron Quotes," LifeQuotesLib.com, http://www. lifequoteslib.com/authors/lord_byron.html.

5. Jeffrey Meyers, ed., *Robert Lowell: Interviews and Memoirs* (Ann Arbor: University of Michigan Press, 1988), 49.

Chapter 1

6. Ralph Waldo Emerson, *The Later Lectures of Ralph Waldo Emerson, 1843-1871, Volume 2: 1855-1871*, ed. Ronald A. Bosco and Joel Myerson (Athens, GA: University of Georgia Press, 2010), 142.

7. U. S. Andersen, *The Magic in Your Mind* (Important Books, 2012), 7.

8. "Theodore Roethke Quotes," Quotesome, https://www. quotesome.com/authors/theodore-roethke/quotes.

9   Christian McEwen, *World Enough and Time: On Creativity and Slowing Down* (New Hampshire: Bauhan Publishing, 2011), 204.

10   "Little Things," PoemHunter.com, http://poemhunter.com/poem/little-things/.

11   Joseph Murphy, *The Miracles of Your Mind* (Carlsbad, CA: Hay House, 1956).

12   Austin Kleon, *Steal Like an Artist: 10 Things Nobody Told You About Being Creative* (New York: Workman Publishing, 2012), 67.

13   Papaji (H. W. L. Poonja), *Wake Up and Roar* (Boulder, CO: Sounds True, 2007).

14   Eckhart Tolle, *Stillness Speaks* (Vancouver, Canada: Namaste Publishing, 2003).

15   David R. Hawkins, *Reality and Subjectivity* (Sedona, AZ: Veritas Publishing, 2003).

16   Papaji, *Wake Up and Roar.*

17   Dr. Wayne W. Dyer, *Being in Balance: 9 Principles for Creating Habits to Match Your Desires* (Carlsbad, CA: Hay House, 2006).

18   Srikumar S. Rao, *Happiness at Work: Be Resilient, Motivated, and Successful—No Matter What* (New York: McGraw-Hill, 2010).

19   Jeanne de Salzman, *Reality of Being* (Boston: Shambala Publishing, 2010).

20   Tolle, *Stillness Speaks.*

21   Scott Jeffrey, *Creativity Revealed: Discovering the Source of Inspiration* (Kingston, NY: Creative Crayon Publishing, 2008).

Chapter 2

22 Julia Cameron, *The Artist's Way: A Spiritual Path to Higher Creativity* (New York: Penguin Putnam, Inc., 2002).

23 Michael Mirdad, *You're Not Going Crazy... You're Just Waking Up: The Five Stages of Soul Transformation Process* (Bellingham, WA: Grail Press, 2011).

24 Orison Swett Marden, *He Can Who Thinks He Can: And Other Papers on Success in Life* (Whitefish, MT: Kessinger Publishing, 2003).

25 "Henry David Thoreau Quotes," ThinkExist.com, http://think exist.com/quotation/most_men_lead_lives_of_quiet_ desperation_and_go/209139.html.

26 Marden, *He Can Who Thinks He Can.*

27 "Wisdom of Heraclitus," EmpHasise, http://enghweeong. wordpress.com/2009/01/07/wisdom-of-heraclitus/.

28 Neville Goddard, *Neville Goddard Collection* (Charleston, SC: Createspace, 2013).

29 "Rabindranath Tagore Quotes," BrainyQuote, http://www. brainyquote.com/quotes/authors/r/rabindranath_tagore. html.

30 "Sometimes," Bartleby.com, http://www.bartleby.com/104/92. html.

31 Taro Gold, *Open Your Mind, Open Your Life: A Book of Eastern Wisdom* (Lionstead Press, 2002).

32 Marden, *He Can Who Thinks He Can.*

33 *Transcript: General Assembly, June 3, 1980*, State of Illinois House of Representatives, http://www.ilga.gov/house/ transcripts/htrans81/HT060380.pdf.

34 "Robert Louis Stevenson > Quotes," GoodReads, http:// www.goodreads.com/author/quotes/854076.Robert_Louis_ Stevenson.

Chapter 3

35 "Fran Lebowitz Quotes," BrainyQuote, http://www. brainyquote.com/quotes/authors/f/fran_lebowitz.html.

36 "Life Quotes," ThinkExist.com, http://thinkexist.com/ quotations/Life.

37 Orison Swett Marden, *He Can Who Thinks He Can: And Other Papers on Success in Life* (Whitefish, MT: Kessinger Publishing, 2003).

38 U. S. Andersen, *The Magic in Your Mind* (Important Books, 2012), 8

39 "William Shakespeare Quotes," BrainyQuote, http://www. brainyquote.com/quotes/authors/w/william_shakespeare. html.

40 Vernon Howard, *The Power of Your Supermind* (New Jersey: Prentice Hall, 1975).

41 "Abraham Lincoln Quotes," BrainyQuote, http://www. brainyquote.com/quotes/authors/a/abraham_lincoln.html.

42 "Albert Einstein Quotes," GoodReads, http://www.goodreads. com/author/quotes/9810.Albert_Einstein.

43 "Hometown Quotes," ThinkExist.com, http://thinkexist.com/ quotes/with/keyword/hometown/.

44 "Henry David Thoreau Quotes," BrainyQuote, http://www.brainyquote.com/quotes/authors/h/ henry_david_thoreau.html.

45 "Robert Frost Quotes," BrainyQuote, http://www.brainyquote. com/quotes/authors/r/robert_frost.html.

46 "Quotations by Author: L. L. Henderson," The Quotations Page, http://www.quotationspage.com/quotes/L._L._Henderson/.

47 "Abraham Lincoln Quotes," ThinkExist.com, http://thinkexist. com/quotes/abraham_lincoln/.

48 Joseph Murphy, *The Miracles of Your Mind* (Carlsbad, CA: Hay House, 1956).

49 James Hetfield, Lars Ulrich, Kirk Hammett (Metallica), "Bleeding Me," 1996.

50 "Lao Tzu Quotes," BrainyQuotes, http://www.brainyquote. com/quotes/authors/l/lao_tzu.html.

51 "Henry David Thoreau Quotes," GoodReads, http://www. goodreads.com/author/quotes/10264.Henry_David_Thoreau.

52 "Napoleon Hill Quotes," BrainyQuote, http://www. brainyquote.com/quotes/authors/n/napoleon_hill.html.

53 "William Blake Quotes," BrainyQuote, http://www. brainyquote.com/quotes/authors/w/william_blake.html.

54 Marden, *He Can Who Thinks He Can.*

55 Ernest Holmes, *How to Use the Science of Mind: Principle in Practice* (Science of Mind Publishing, 1984)

56 "Publilius Syrus Quotes," Famous Quotes, http://www. allfamousquotes.net/publilius-syrus-quotes/.

57 Scott Jeffrey, *Creativity Revealed: Discovering the Source of Inspiration* (Kingston, NY: Creative Crayon Publishing, 2008)

58 Taro Gold, *Open Your Mind, Open Your Life: A Book of Eastern Wisdom* (Lionstead Press, 2002).

59 Papaji (H. W. L. Poonja), *Wake Up and Roar* (Boulder, CO: Sounds True, 2007).

60 Howard, *The Power of Your Supermind.*

61 Marden, *He Can Who Thinks He Can.*

62 "Guy Debord > Quotes," Good Reads, http://www.goodreads. com/author/quotes/15819.Guy_Debord.

63 Julia Cameron, *The Artist's Way: A Spiritual Path to Higher Creativity* (New York: Penguin Putnam, Inc., 2002).

64 "Quotes about Syrus, Publilius," QuotationsBook, http://quotationsbook.com/quotes/author/7102/page=3/#sthash.EYUiSIqI.dpbs.

65 Marden, *He Can Who Thinks He Can.*

66 "Riches," MoreQuotations.com, http://morequotations.com/Quotations/riches.html.

67 Andersen, *The Magic in Your Mind.*

68 Fenwicke L. Holmes, *Being and Becoming: A Book of Lessons in the Science of Mind Showing How to Find the Personal Spirit* (Whitefish, MT: Kessinger Publishing, 2004).

Chapter 4

69 "Al Capone Quotes," BrainyQuote, http://www.brainyquote.com/quotes/authors/a/al_capone.html.

70 Chris Guillebeau, *The Art of Non-Conformity: Set Your Own Rules, Live the Life You Want, and Change the World* (New York: Perigee, 2010).

71 "Lucky Luciano Quotes & Sayings," SearchQuotes, http://www.searchquotes.com/quotes/author/Lucky_Luciano/.

72 Thomas J. Peters and Robert H. Waterman, *In Search of Excellence: Lessons from America's Best-Run Companies* (New York: HarperCollins, 2004).

73 "Kevin Stirtz ASG," SelfGrowth.com, http://www.selfgrowth.com/experts/kevin_stirtz.html.

74 Larry Winget, *It's Called Work for a Reason!: Your Success Is Your Own Damn Fault* (New York: Gotham Books, 2007), 192.

75 "Customer Service Quotes," AmazingServiceGuy.com, http://amazingserviceguy.com/customer-service-quotes-page-1/.

76 John Greathouse, "23 Leadership Tips From Oprah Winfrey," *Forbes*, September 27, 2012, http://www.forbes.com/sites/

johngreathouse/2012/09/27/23-leadership-tips-from-oprah-winfrey/3/.

77   "The Inaugural Address of FDR," ABC News, http://abcnews.
     go.com/Politics/OTUS/inaugural-address-franklin-roosevelt/
     story?id=18162792&page=5.

78   "Steve Jobs Quotes," BrainyQuote, http://www.brainyquote.
     com/quotes/authors/s/steve_jobs_3.html.

79   "Donald Trump Quotes," BrainyQuote, http://www.
     brainyquote.com/quotes/authors/d/donald_trump.html.

80   "Michael J. Gelb Quotes," ThinkExist.com, http://thinkexist.
     com/quotes/Michael_J._Gelb/.

81   "Thomas A. Edison Quotes," BrainyQuote, http://www.
     brainyquote.com/quotes/authors/t/thomas_a_edison.html.

82   "You're Not the Only Pebble on the Beach," Library of
     Congress, http://www.loc.gov/item/ihas.100005042.

83   "Donnie Brasco: Quotes," IMDb, http://www.imdb.com/title/
     tt0119008/quotes.

84   "Publilius Syrus Quotes," BrainyQuote, http://www.
     brainyquote.com/quotes/authors/p/publilius_syrus_2.html.

85   Eckhart Tolle, Stillness Speaks (Vancouver, Canada: Namaste
     Publishing, 2003).

86   Michael L. Ray, The Highest Goal: The Secret That Sustains You
     in Every Moment (San Francisco: Berrett-Koehler Publishing,
     Inc., 2004).

87   "Rebecca West Quotes," BrainyQuote, http://www.brainy
     quote.com/quotes/authors/r/rebecca_west.html.

88   Srikumar S. Rao, Happiness at Work: Be Resilient, Motivated,
     and Successful—No Matter What (New York: McGraw-Hill,
     2010).

89 "Proverb Quotes," ThinkExist.com, http://thinkexist.com/quotation/when_you_reach_the_top-keep_climbing/149253.html.

90 Bob Greene, *The 50 Year Dash: The Feelings, Foibles, and Fears of Being Half a Century Old* (New York: Doubleday, 1997).

Chapter 5

91 "Quotes about Lacroix, Christian," Quotations Book, http://quotationsbook.com/quotes/author/4179/#sthash.VvL1epgw.dpbs.

92 Matthew E. May, *In Pursuit of Elegance: Why the Best Ideas Have Something Missing* (New York: Broadway Books, 2009).

93 May, *In Pursuit of Elegance.*

94 May, *In Pursuit of Elegance.*

95 "Jon Franklin Quotes and Quotations," Famous Quotes & Authors, http://famousquotesandauthors.com/authors/jon_franklin_quotes.html.

Chapter 6

96 William Wordsworth, "Resolution and Independence," Bartleby.com, http://www.bartleby.com/145/ww202.html.

97 Anam Thubten, *No Self, No Problem* (Ithaca, NY: Snow Lion Publications, 2009).

98 "Quotations by Henry David Thoreau," Dictionary.com, http://quotes.dictionary.com/with_thinking_we_may_be_beside_ourselves_in.

99 Vernon Howard, *The Power of Your Supermind* (New Jersey: Prentice Hall, 1975).

100 "Spectator Quotes," ThinkExist.com, http://thinkexist.com/quotes/with/keyword/spectator/3.html.

101 Taro Gold, *Open Your Mind, Open Your Life: A Book of Eastern Wisdom* (Lionstead Press, 2002).

102 *The Sayings of Buddha* (USA: Piccadilly Inc., by arrangement with Hugh L. Levin LLC., 2011).

Chapter 7

103 "Ralph Waldo Emerson Quotes," BrainyQuote, http://www.brainyquote.com/quotes/authors/r/ralph_waldo_emerson_3.html.

104 "Quotation by Honoré De Balzac," Dictionary.com Quotes, http://quotes.dictionary.com/Thought_is_a_key_to_all_treasures_the.

105 *The Sayings of Buddha* (USA: Piccadilly Inc., by arrangement with Hugh L. Levin, LLC., 2011).

106 Taro Gold, *Living Wabi Sabi: The True Beauty of Your Life* (Lionstead Press, 2004).

107 Eckhart Tolle, *Stillness Speaks* (Vancouver, Canada: Namaste Publishing, 2003).

108 *The Sayings of Buddha.*

109 Ernest Holmes, *The Art of Life* (New York: Penguin Group, 2004).

110 Sakyong Mipham, *Ruling Your World: Ancient Strategies for Modern Life* (New York: Morgan Road Books, 2005).

111 Michael Singer, *The Untethered Soul* (Oakland, CA: New Harbinger Publications, 2007).

112 Neville Goddard, *Feeling Is the Secret* (Beta Nu Publishing, 2007).

113 Orison Swett Marden, *Change the Thought, Change the Man* (Whitefish, MT: Kessinger Publishing, 2010).

114 Saint Germain, *The "I Am" Discourses, Vol. 3* (Schaumberg, IL: Saint Germain Press, 2010).

[115] Henry Van Dyke, "Thoughts Are Things," Leksurfer, http://leksurfer.com/thoughts-are-things.

[116] "Seneca," Bartleby.com, http://www.bartleby.com/348/authors/487.html.

[117] "Quotation by Henry David Thoreau," Dictionary.com, http://quotes.dictionary.com/with_thinking_we_may_be_beside_ourselves_in.

[118] Venice Bloodworth, *Key To Yourself* (Beta Nu Publiishing, 2008).

[119] Anam Thubten, *No Self, No Problem* (Ithaca, NY: Snow Lion Publications, 2009).

Chapter 8

[120] Ernest Holmes, *A New Design for Living* (New York: The Penguin Group, 2010).

[121] Bruce Lipton, *Biology of Belief: Unleashing the Power of Consciousness, Matter, and Miracles* (Carlsbad, CA: Hay House, Inc., 2005).

[122] Chris Guillebeau, *The Art of Non-Conformity: Set Your Own Rules, Live the Life You Want, and Change the World* (New York: Perigee, 2010).

[123] Vernon Howard, *The Power of Esoterics* (Pine, AZ: New Life Foundation, 1999).

[124] The Sayings of Buddha (USA: Piccadilly Inc., by arrangement of Hugh L. Levin LLC., 2011).

[125] Howard, *The Power of Esoterics.*

[126] Vernon Howard, *Esoteric Mind Power* (Pine, AZ: New Life Foundation, 1994).

[127] Samuel A. Schreiner, Jr., *The Concord Quartet: Alcott, Emerson, Hawthorne, Thoreau and the Friendship That Freed*

the *American Mind* (Hoboken, NJ: John Wiley & Sons, Inc., 2010).

128 "French Proverb Quotes," ThinkExist.com, http://thinkexist. com/quotation/hope_is_the_dream_of_a_soul_awake/ 260939.html.

129 Dr. Joseph Murphy, *Believe in Yourself* (Carlsbad, CA: Hay House, 1956).

130 David R. Hawkins, *Reality and Subjectivity* (Sedona, AZ: Veritas Publishing, 2003).

Chapter 9

131 "Publilius Syrus Quotes," Famous Quotes, http://www. allfamousquotes.net/publilius-syrus-quotes/.

132 Fenwicke L. Holmes, *Being and Becoming: A Book of Lessons in the Science of Mind Showing How to Find the Personal Spirit* (Whitefish, MT: Kessinger Publishing, 2004).

133 Orison Swett Marden, *He Can Who Thinks He Can: And Other Papers on Success in Life* (Whitefish, MT: Kessinger Publishing, 2003).

134 Paul William, *Das Energi.*

135 "Albert Einstein Quotes," BrainyQuote, http://www. brainyquote.com/quotes/authors/a/albert_einstein.html.

136 "Publilius Syrus Quotes," BrainyQuote, http://www. brainyquote.com/quotes/authors/p/publilius_syrus.html.

137 "Never Give Up Quotes," BrainyQuote, http://www.brainy quote.com/quotes/keywords/never_give_up.html.

138 Scott Jeffrey, *Journey to the Impossible: Designing an Extraordinary Life* (New York: Creative Crayon Publishing, 2002).

139 Jeff Foster, *An Extraordinary Absence: Liberation in the Midst of a Very Ordinary Life* (Salisbury, Wiltshire, United Kingdom: Non-Duality Press, 2009).

140 Michael Mirdad, *You're Not Going Crazy... You're Just Waking Up: The Five Stages of Soul Transformation Process* (Bellingham, WA: Grail Press, 2011).

141 "Thoughts on the Business of Life," Forbes.com, http://thoughts.forbes.com/thoughts/health-charles-lamb-how-sickness-enlarges.

142 David R. Hawkins, *Transcending the Levels of Consciousness: The Stairway to Enlightenment* (West Sedona, AZ: Veritas Publishing, 2006).

143 "Juvenal (Decimus Junius Juvenal)," GIGA Quotes, http://www.giga-usa.com/quotes/authors/juvenal_a005.htm.

144 "Quotes," Corruptico, http://corruptico.com/quotes.

145 Dr. Joe Dispenza, *Breaking the Habit of Being Yourself: How to Lose Your Mind and Create a New One* (Carlsbad, CA: Hay House, 2012).

146 Ralph Waldo Trine, *Thoughts I Met On The Highway* (New York: Dodd, Mead & Company, 1919).

147 "Ralph Browning Hamilton > Quotes > Quotable Quotes," GoodReads, http://www.goodreads.com/quotes/289683-i-walked-a-mile-with-pleasure-she-chatted-all-the.

Chapter 10

148 Ernest Holmes, *This Thing Called You* (New York: Jeremy P. Tarcher/Penguin, 1948).

149 Dr. Joseph Murphy, *Believe in Yourself* (Carlsbad, CA: Hay House, 1956).

150 Neville Goddard, *Neville Goddard Collection* (Charleston, SC: Createspace, 2013).

151 Goddard, *Neville Goddard Collection.*

152 Vernon Howard, *Esoteric Mind Power* (Pine, AZ: New Life Foundation, 1999)

153 Murphy, *Believe in Yourself.*

154 Neville Goddard, *Your Faith Is Your Fortune* (Seattle, WA: Pacific Publishing Studio, 2010).

155 Goddard, *Neville Goddard Collection.*

156 Don Miguel Ruiz and Don Jose Ruiz with Janet Mills, *The Fifth Agreement: A Practical Guide to Self-Mastery* (San Rafael, CA: Amber-Allen Publishing, Inc., 2010).

157 Saint Germain, *The "I Am" Discourses, Vol. 3* (Schaumberg, IL: Saint Germain Press, 2010).

Chapter 11

158 "John Wooden Quotes," BrainyQuote, http://www.brainyquote.com/quotes/authors/j/john_wooden.html.

159 "Flattery," MoreQuotations.com, http://www.morequotations.com/Quotations/flattery.html.

160 Pete Wilson, "False Praise and Distorted Criticism," Church Leaders, http://www.churchleaders.com/outreach-missions/outreach-missions-blogs/158317-pete_wilson_false_praise_and_distorted_criticism.html.

161 "Quotations by Washington Irving," Dictionary.com, http://quotes.dictionary.com/Whenever_a_mans_friends_begin_to_compliment_him.

162 "Dale Carnegie Quotes," GoodReads, http://www.goodreads.com/author/quotes/3317.Dale_Carnegie.

163 Fenwicke L. Holmes, *Being and Becoming: A Book of Lessons in the Science of Mind Showing How to Find the Personal Spirit* (Whitefish, MT: Kessinger Publishing, 2004).

164 "Thomas Wolfe Quotes," BrainyQuote, http://www. brainyquote.com/quotes/authors/t/thomas_wolfe.html.

165 *The Sayings of Buddha.*

166 "Publilius Syrus Quotes," BrainyQuote, http://www. brainyquote.com/quotes/authors/p/publilius_syrus_3.html.

167 Taro Gold, *Open Your Mind, Open Your Life: A Book of Eastern Wisdom* (Lionstead Press, 2002).

168 Ernest Holmes, *The Science of Mind* (Radford, VA: Wilder Publications, 2010).

169 John Randolph Price, *Nothing Is Too Good to Be True* (Carlsbad, CA: Hay House, Inc., 2003).

170 David R. Hawkins, *The Eye of the I: From Which Nothing Is Hidden* (West Sedona, AZ: Veritas Publishing).

171 "Mencken's Law," *The Barnes & Noble Review,* August 12, 2013, http://bnreview.barnesandnoble.com/t5/Daybook/ Mencken-s-Law/ba-p/10179.

172 John Selby, *Quiet Your Mind* (Novato, CA: New World Library, 2004).

173 "François de La Rochefoucauld," Wikiquote, http://en. wikiquote.org/wiki/François_de_La_Rochefoucauld.

174 "Publilius Syrus," The Quotations Page, http://www. quotationspage.com/quotes/Publilius_Syrus/31.

175 Paul Williams, *Das Energi.*

176 "Thomas A. Edison Quotes," BrainyQuote, http://www. brainyquote.com/quotes/authors/t/thomas_a_edison_2.html.

177 David R. Hawkins, *Dissolving the Ego, Realizing the Self* (Carlsbad, CA: Hay House, 2011).

178 "Ralph Waldo Emerson Quote," iWise.com, http://www.iwise. com/mY079.

179 "Sydney Smith Quotes," BrainyQuote, http://www.brainy quote.com/quotes/authors/s/sydney_smith_2.html.

180 Ken Wilber, *No Boundary: Eastern and Western Approaches to Personal Growth* (Boston: Shambala Publications, Inc., 2001), 25.

181 "Charles Lamb Quotes," BrainyQuote, http://www.brainyquote.com/quotes/authors/c/charles_lamb_2.html.

182 "Arthur Schopenhauer Quotes," BrainyQuote, http://www.brainyquote.com/quotes/authors/a/arthur_schopenhauer.html.

183 "Jean-Jacques Rousseau Quotes," BrainyQuote, http://www.brainyquote.com/quotes/authors/j/jeanjacques_rousseau.html.

184 Stephen Mitchell, *Tao Te Ching* (New York: Harper & Row, 1988).

185 "Claude Bernard Quotes," BrainyQuote, http://www.brainyquote.com/quotes/authors/c/claude_bernard.html.

186 "Death," MoreQuotations.com, http://www.morequotations.com/Quotations/death.html.

187 Anam Thubten, *No Self, No Problem* (Ithaca, NY: Snow Lion Publications, 2009).

188 David R. Hawkins, *The Eye of the I: From Which Nothing Is Hidden* (West Sedona, AZ: Veritas Publishing, 2001).

189 Krishnamurti, *Freedom from the Known* (New York: HarperCollins Publishers, 1969)

190 Deepak Chopra, *Creating Affluence: The A-to-Z Steps to a Richer Life* (Quantum Publications Inc., 1992).

191 David R. Hawkins, *Transcending the Levels of Consciousness: The Stairway to Enlightenment* (West Sedona, Arizona: Veritas Publishing, 2006).

192 Anam Thubten, *No Self, No Problem* (Ithaca, NY: Snow Lion Publications, 2009).

[193] Taro Gold, *Living Wabi Sabi: The True Beauty of Your Life* (Lionstead Press, 2004).

Chapter 12

[194] "Moliere Quotes," ThinkExist.com, http://thinkexist. com/quotation/nearly_all_men_die_of_their_remedies-and_not_of/148747.html.
[195] *The Sayings of Buddha* (USA: Piccadilly, Inc., by arrangement with Hugh L. Levin LLC., 2011).
[196] Taro Gold, *Open Your Mind, Open Your Life: A Book of Eastern Wisdom* (Lionstead Press, 2002).
[197] Venice Bloodworth, *Key To Yourself* (Beta Nu Publiishing, 2008).
[198] Bruce Lipton, *Biology of Belief: Unleashing the Power of Consciousness, Matter, and Miracles* (Carlsbad, CA: Hay House, Inc., 2005).
[199] Ernest Holmes, *Discover a Richer Life* (New York: Penguin Group, 1961).
[200] Scott Jeffrey, *Creativity Revealed: Discovering the Source of Inspiration* (Kingston, NY: Creative Crayon Publishing, 2008).
[201] John Randolph Price, *Nothing Is Too Good to Be True* (Carlsbad, CA: Hay House, Inc., 2003).
[202] Paramahansa Yogananda, *Living Fearlessly: Bringing Out Your Inner Soul Strength* (Los Angeles, CA: Self-Realization Fellowship, 2003).
[203] Bloodworth, *Key to Yourself.*
[204] Dr. Wayne Dyer, *Change Your Thoughts—Change Your Life: Living the Wisdom of the Tao* (Carlsbad, CA: Hay House, 2007).
[205] Ramón Stevens, *Conscious Life: Creating Your Reality* (Pepperwood Press, 2009, 1991).

206 Dr. John Efferiedes, *Parade Magazine.*

· 207 Deepak Chopra, *Power, Freedom, and Grace: Living from the Source of Lasting Happiness* (San Rafael, CA: Amber-Allen Publishing, Inc., 2006).

208 "Quotes about Linnaeus, Carolus," Quotations Book, http://quotationsbook.com/quotes/author/4436/#sthash. vmFr51K3.dpbs.

209 Orison Swett Marden, *Change the Thought, Change the Man* (Whitefish, MT: Kessinger Publising, 2010).

Chapter 13

210 David R. Hawkins, *Discovery of the Presence of God: Devotional NonDuality* (Hay House, Inc., 2007).

211 David R. Hawkins, *Discovery of the Presence of God: Devotional NonDuality* (Hay House, Inc., 2007).

212 "Thinkexist.com," http://thinkexist.com/quotation/ before_enlightenment

213 David R. Hawkins, *Dissolving the Ego Realizing the Self: Contemplations from the Teachings of David R. Hawkins, M.D., Ph.D* (Hay House, Inc., 2011)

214 "Poemhunter.com," poemhunter.com>Poems>Louis Untermeyer, http//www.poemhunter.com/poem/prayer-110.

215 David R. Hawkins, *Along the Path to Enlightenment, 365 Daily Reflections from David R. Hawkins* (Hay House, Inc., 2011).

216 Taro Gold, *Open Your Mind, Open Your Life: A Book of Eastern Wisdom* (Lionstead Press, 2002).

217 Taro Gold, *Open Your Mind, Open Your Life: A Book of Eastern Wisdom* (Lionstead Press, 2002).

218 "Famous Quotes About," www.famousquotesabout.com/ quote/An-object-in-possession/52956.

[219] David R. Hawkins, *Along the Path to Enlightenment, 365 Daily Reflections from David R. Hawkins* (Hay House, Inc. 2011).

Chapter 14

[220] Vernon Howard, *The Power of Esoterics* (Pine, AZ: New Life Foundation, 1999).
[221] *The Sayings of Buddha* (USA: Piccadilly Inc., by arrangement with Hugh L. Levin, LLC., 2011).
[222] Eckhart Tolle, *Stillness Speaks* (Vancouver, Canada: Namaste Publishing, 2003).
[223] *The Sayings of Buddha.*
[224] Taro Gold, *Living Wabi Sabi: The True Beauty of Your Life* (Lionstead Press, 2004).

Chapter 15

[225] Orison Swett Marden, *He Can Who Thinks He Can: And Other Papers on Success in Life* (Whitefish, MT: Kessinger Publishing, 2003).
[226] Michael L. Ray, *The Highest Goal: The Secret That Sustains You in Every Moment* (San Francisco: Berrett-Koehler Publishing, Inc., 2004).
[227] "Essays XVI. New England Reformers," Bartleby.com, http://www.bartleby.com/5/116.html.

Chapter 16

[228] Ernest Holmes, *It's Up to You* (New York: Jeremy P. Tarcher/Penguin, 2010).
[229] U. S. Andersen, *The Magic in Your Mind* (Important Books, 2012).

230 Vernon Howard, *The Power of Esoterics* (Pine, AZ: New Life Foundation, 1999).

231 Stephen Cope, *The Great Work of Your Life: A Guide for the Journey to Your True Calling* (New York: Bantam Books, 2012).

232 "George Allen, Sr. Quotes," BrainyQuote, http://www.brainyquote.com/quotes/authors/g/george_allen_sr.html.

233 "Ralph Waldo Emerson Quotes," Search Quotes, http://www.searchquotes.com/quotation/No_one_can_cheat_you_out_of_ultimate_success_but_yourself./300883/.

234 Orison Swett Marden, *He Can Who Thinks He Can: And Other Papers on Success in Life* (Whitefish, MT: Kessinger Publishing, 2003).

235 "Thoreau," Bartleby.com, http://www.bartleby.com/348/authors/554.html.

236 "Epictetus Quotes," BrainyQuote, http://www.brainyquote.com/quotes/authors/e/epictetus_3.html.

237 Marden, *He Can Who Thinks He Can.*

238 Orison Swett Marden, *Change the Thought, Change the Man* (Whitefish, MT: Kessinger Publishing, 2010).

Chapter 17

239 Papaji (H. W. L. Poonja), *Wake Up and Roar* (Boulder, CO: Sounds True, 2007).

240 Chris Guillebeau, *The Art of Non-Conformity: Set Your Own Rules, Live the Life You Want, and Change the World* (New York: Perigee, 2010).

241 Dzogchen Ponlop, *The Rebel Buddha: On the Road to Freedom* (Boston: Shambala Publications, 2010).

242 Papaji, *Wake Up and Roar.*

[243] "Robert Louis Stevenson Quotes," BrainyQuote, http://www.brainyquote.com/quotes/authors/r/robert_louis_stevenson.html.

[244] Ernest Holmes, *The Hidden Power of the Bible: What* Science of the Mind *Reveals About the Bible and You* (New York: The Penguin Group, 2005).

[245] Vernon Howard, *The Power of Your Supermind* (New Jersey: Prentice Hall, 1975).

[246] Don Miguel Ruiz, *The Four Agreements: A Toltec Wisdom Book* (San Rafael, CA: Amber-Allen Publishing, 1999).

[247] U. S. Andersen, *The Magic in Your Mind* (Important Books, 2012).

[248] David R. Hawkins, *Dissolving the Ego, Realizing the Self* (Carlsbad, CA: Hay House, 2011).

[249] Orison Swett Marden, *He Can Who Thinks He Can: And Other Papers on Success in Life* (Whitefish, MT: Kessinger Publishing, 2003).

[250] William Ellery Channing, "Spiritual Freedom," American Unitarian Conference, http://www.americanunitarian.org/spiritualfreedom.htm.

Chapter 18

[251] "Paul Gardner > Quotes > Quotable Quote," GoodReads, http://www.goodreads.com/quotes/23976-a-painting-is-never-finished---it-simply-stops-in.

[252] Don Miguel Ruiz, *The Four Agreements: A Toltec Wisdom Book* (San Rafael, CA: Amber-Allen Publishing, 1999).

[253] Ramana Maharishi, Annamalai Swami, Vasistha, Sankara, Nisargadatta Maharaj, Muruganar, and Sadhu Om, *The Seven Steps to Awakening* (The Freedom Religion Press, 2010).

[254] *The Seven Steps to Awakening.*

255 U. S. Andersen, *The Magic in Your Mind* (Important Books, 2012).

256 Neville Goddard, *Neville Goddard Collection* (Charleston, SC: Createspace, 2013).

257 Julia Cameron, *The Artist's Way: A Spiritual Path to Higher Creativity* (New York: Penguin Putnam, Inc., 2002).

258 Thubten, *No Self, No Problem.*

259 Ernest Holmes, *The Art of Life* (New York: Penguin Group, 2004).

260 Andersen, *The Magic in Your Mind.*

261 "Max Planck," Wikiquote, http://en.wikiquote.org/wiki/Max_Planck.

262 Andersen, *The Magic in Your Mind.*

263 Deepak Chopra, *Unconditional Life: Discovering the Power to Fulfill Your Dreams* (New York: Bantam Book, 1991).

264 Dr. Wayne Dyer, *Change Your Thoughts—Change Your Life: Living the Wisdom of the Tao* (Carlsbad, CA: Hay House, 2007).

265 Papaji (H. W. L. Poonja), *Wake Up and Roar* (Boulder, CO: Sounds True, 2007).

266 Jacob Liberman, with Erik Liberman, *Wisdom from an Empty Mind* (Empty Mind Publications, 2001).

7978991R00167

Made in the USA
San Bernardino, CA
23 January 2014